Commentaries
on the
REPUBLIC

FREDERICK HEADEN

NEWMAN SPRINGS PUBLISHING
320 Broad Street
Red Bank, NJ 07701

First originally published by Newman Springs Publishing 2023

ISBN 978-1-68498-894-5 (Paperback)
ISBN 978-1-68498-895-2 (Digital)

Printed in the United States of America

To Susan, before I ever met you, the mere thought of you was an inspiration.

"It has been frequently remarked, that it seems to have been reserved to the people of this country, by their conduct and example, to decide the important question, whether societies of men are really capable or not, of establishing good government from reflection and choice, or whether they are forever destined to depend, for their political constitutions, on accident and force."

—Alexander Hamilton

"Do you not think that an Angel rides in the whirlwind and directs this Storm?"

—John Page, writing to Thomas Jefferson shortly after the Declaration of Independence was published to express confidence in the prospects of the fledgling nation.

"I predict future happiness for Americans, if they can prevent the government from wasting the labors of the people under the pretense of taking care of them."

—Thomas Jefferson

"If I were to try to read, much less answer, all the attacks made on me, this shop might as well be closed for any other business. I do the very best I know how—the very best I can; and I mean to keep doing so until the end. If the end brings me out all right, what's said against me won't amount to anything. If the end brings me out wrong, ten angels swearing I was right would make no difference."

—Abraham Lincoln

Contents

Introduction..vii

Part 1
Book Reviews
    Six Quiet Men Who Molded Postwar World 3
    A Novel Plan for Post-Apartheid South Africa 7
    Black Leadership in American Society...................................11
    Jackson: Motivation and the Message 15
    Bush Ought to Be "Thinking about America" 18
    Cutting the Court's Hold on Regulation...............................22
    Will South Africa Embrace Free-Market System?.................25
    Judicial Intervention Has Mixed Track Record.....................29
    Civil Rights Issues More Divisive Than Ever.......................33
    Setting Realistic Goals in the War on Drugs 37
    Racial Classifications? Try the Human Race..........................41
    Addressing the Decline of Shared Values..............................45
    The Sad Irony of the Civil Rights Movement 48
    Racism: Civil Rights and Moral Wrongs..............................52

Part 2
Voices Columns
    Election Affirmed Founders' Wisdom...................................59
    Overburdened Taxpayers Deserve Relief 62
    "Leaders" Let Down Black Americans..................................65
    Courts Should Read Law, Not Write Policy 68

Restore Fairness to Heart of Civil Rights Fight 70
America Must Defend Western Traditions 72
For America, Life Isn't Completely New 75

Part 3
Miscellaneous Commentaries
Liberals' Case Against Bork Falls Short 81
Thomas' Opponents Show Their True Colors......................85
Media Overstate Problem in Iraq Downplay Progress 88
Obamacare Will Stretch the Government's
    Tentacles Too Far 90

Part 4
Postscript
The Unpublished Column..95

Introduction

Ripples in a pond, the pond of one's life, often reverberate in ways not discernible or understood at the time. Only in retrospect are they to be seen clearly. One such instance occurred in my life on a cold, winter evening in February of 1987 in downtown Detroit. I was having dinner with Thomas J. Bray (the former editorial page editor of *The Detroit News*). I had expressed an interest in joining his staff (having admired for some time his, and their, work), and he was considerate enough to invite me to dinner to explore that interest. Possessed of a keen intellect, Tom had assembled an extraordinarily talented group of editorial writers:

- Tony Snow, who was deputy editorial page editor and later would serve as a speechwriter for President George H. W. Bush; as the host of *Fox News Sunday* when it was one of the finest news programs on television; he later would serve as White House Press Secretary in the administration of President George W. Bush. Sadly, colon cancer would cut Tony's life short at the age of fifty-three while his career was still on an ascending trajectory.
- Jeffrey Hadden—a deputy editorial page editor in waiting whose talent as a writer and keen knowledge of our nation's origins were exemplified by a series of splendid essays he penned about the Founding Fathers; the essays later would win well-deserved recognition from the Commission on the Bicentennial of the United States Constitution.
- Ted Douglas, whose expertise lay in international and military affairs.

- Richard Burr, whose duties included overseeing book reviews that *The Detroit News* published each Thursday on the page opposite its editorial page.
- Draper Hill—the long-time editorial page cartoonist who could convey more with a cartoon than could the average individual with the proverbial thousand words. He had, among other talents, an unparalleled ability to depict Detroit's long-time mayor: Coleman Young.

* * * *

The next morning, I arrived at *The Detroit News* building and reported for work, literally. Tom did not believe in traditional job interviews. The best measure of one's ability do the work of editorial writing was to have one write editorials. So I was shown to a cubicle with a computer. A short time later, Tom stopped by with several news clippings that he handed me. He informed me that my assignment, which I was to complete before going to lunch with Tony Snow, was to read the news clippings and compose an editorial. This process was repeated that afternoon when Tony and I returned from lunch. I still recall feeling both surprised and gratified when one of my nervously composed compositions appeared as an editorial the following morning.

Ultimately, personal circumstances would preclude any formal affiliation between me and *The Detroit News*' editorial staff. However, at a follow-up luncheon with Tom in Lansing, I mentioned having recently finished reading an interesting book. He immediately suggested that I write a review of the book and submit it to Richard Burr. I did, and it was published in March of 1987.

Thus began a nearly nine-year stint during which Richard, from time to time, would contact me about a book which he thought I might have an interest in reviewing. He would send me a copy of the book, and several weeks later, I would send him the written review. It was a wonderful opportunity, particularly since many of the books were ones I might never have encountered on my own. I and the other individuals who reviewed books were accorded 1,100–1,200 words in which to share our thoughts with readers about a given book—a generous amount of space on an op-ed page that would be all but unheard of in today's journalism world.

In addition to reviewing books, I was extended the privilege of writing an occasional guest column upon significant issues of the day; the nominations to the U.S. Supreme Court of Robert Bork, in 1987, and Clarence Thomas, in 1991, were two such occasions. I never have forgotten the courtesy, indeed the privilege, Tom Bray extended to me by granting me access to the opinion page of a major daily newspaper.

* * * *

In November of 2000, Mark Nixon, the editorial page editor of the *Lansing State Journal,* issued an invitation to the greater Lansing community for individuals interested in serving as guest columnists for the 2001 calendar year. Mark had extended such an invitation for the previous several years. I was one of seven individuals chosen in November of 2000 to write *Voices* columns during 2001.

Once again, I was given a unique opportunity to work with talented journalists, in this case Mark and deputy editorial page editor, Derek Melot, and to offer opinions to my fellow citizens about important issues of contemporary interest. As luck would have it, I authored both the first and last *Voices* columns of 2001: the former in January of 2001 and the latter six columns later in December of that year. Indeed, my December 2001 *Voices* column truly would be the last one because the *Lansing State Journal* discontinued the program.

That which follows is a compilation of those book reviews, *Voices* columns, and other commentaries (including a heretofore unpublished column found at the conclusion of this book) that I trust will offer readers certain enduring insights about our nation. However, I leave it to my nieces and nephews, and the others of their generation, to decide whether those of my generation preserved for them the republic that Benjamin Franklin said the federal Constitutional Convention of 1787 had given to the American people.

Part 1

Book Reviews

Six Quiet Men Who Molded Postwar World

(The Wise Men: Six Friends and the World They Made by Walter Isaacson and Evan Thomas; Simon and Schuster [1986])*

The *Wise Men* presents a group portraiture of six men who were the chief architects of America's postwar foreign policy: Averell Harriman, Dean Acheson, Robert Lovett, John McCloy, Charles Bohlen, and George Kennan. Because they were extremely private men who preferred to exercise their influence discreetly, their names are not necessarily household words, but the influence they asserted is not to be doubted.

The breadth of their service is impressive. Harriman was a former ambassador to Moscow, governor of New York, and advisor to presidents from Franklin Roosevelt to Ronald Reagan. He first visited the Soviet Union in 1899 when Nicholas II was czar. His last visit was in 1983, at the invitation of Yuri Andropov.

Dean Acheson, an attorney, served as secretary of state under President Truman and played a prominent role in formulating what came to be known as the Truman Doctrine. Robert Lovett was an assistant secretary of war, undersecretary of state, and secretary of defense. John McCloy served as assistant secretary of war, U.S. high commissioner for Germany, and later as president of the Chase Bank. Charles Bohlen, a diplomat, served in various capacities, including ambassador to Paris under President Kennedy.

George Kennan, a foreign-service diplomat, wrote the containment theory for dealing with what he saw as Soviet expansionism. According to Henry Kissinger, Kennan "came as close to authoring the diplomatic doctrine of his era as any diplomat in our history."

The authors offer an insightful look at the Eastern Establishment, of which the Wise Men were exemplars. The Establishment tradition was founded by Elihu Root, who was President McKinley's secretary of war and Theodore Roosevelt's secretary of state. The lineal descendant of the tradition was Henry Stimson, secretary of war under both William Howard Taft and Franklin Roosevelt.

This tradition held that serving the country was a noble cause, a cause to be undertaken by gentlemen with proper respect for civility. For example, in 1929 when a proposal was made to set up a State Department intelligence service, Stimson rejected it by saying that "gentlemen do not read other peoples' mail." McCloy, who along with Lovett, worked for Stimson, later remarked that "I felt a direct current running from Root to Stimson to me."

At first glance, members of the Establishment fit the standard caricature of being carbon copy Wall Street men of money who were "internationalists" in foreign policy outlook. They had known each other socially and professionally for years. And the seeds of elitism were admittedly present.

Kennan, for example, began a book draft in 1938 that said "women in the U.S. tended to be more 'high strung, unsatisfied, flat-chested, and flat-voiced' than those in other countries and would lead more meaningful lives if they returned to 'family picnics, children's parties and the church social'" and that blacks "would be better off if they were 'openly dependent' on the kindness of society." But it is unfair and inaccurate to categorize such men simply as narrow elitists.

The Wise Men took their apprenticeship during the presidency of Franklin Roosevelt and came into their own when Truman became president. The self-assured Roosevelt had operated on his own, but the Wise Men felt they had a duty to counsel the haberdasher from Missouri on the realities of world politics.

They cared passionately about advancing the prospects of America in its new role as postwar world leader, realizing that most

Americans would have little desire to involve the country in international affairs when the war was won. With victory over Nazi Germany and Japan on the horizon, most Americans wanted only "to go to movies and drink Coke," as Harriman put it.

But the Wise Men were already wrestling with Soviet expansionism, the task of rebuilding a war-torn Europe, and how to prudently manage atomic weapons. They had seen America retreat into isolationism after the First World War and were convinced it had been a mistake.

The book reveals that the lives of these men intertwined like strands of whole cloth. For example, Harriman taught Acheson rowing when both were students at Groton. Acheson and McCloy were classmates at Harvard Law School. Lovett's father had served as general counsel to the Southern Pacific Railroad, of which Harriman's father was chairman.

They symbolized an earlier, more elegant age when America's best put their personal interests temporarily aside to promote the nation's interest as they saw it. Both Lovett and McCloy, for example, left successful careers to work for Stimson in the War Department at $10,000 a year. The salary did not greatly concern them because they viewed public service as their duty. (The descendants of the tradition are among us still. To mention but a few: the Bundy brothers, William and McGeorge, served in both the Kennedy and Johnson administrations. William Bundy was the son-in-law of Acheson. McGeorge Bundy assisted in writing Stimson's memoirs. Cyrus Vance was secretary of state under Jimmy Carter. Paul Nitze is an arms negotiator for the Reagan administration.)

Nor were the Wise Men concerned with not being in the public eye. For instance, the authors note "[t]here are fifty-two monuments or outdoor statues in Washington honoring a wide assortment of long-forgotten as well as famous figures, but in the public spaces of the capital there is not so much as a park bench named after Dean Acheson."

As a group—with the exception of Harriman—they disdained politics, preferring instead to let the politicians come to them. In December 1960, President-elect Kennedy offered Lovett his choice of three cabinet posts: secretary of state, secretary of defense, or secretary of the treasury. Lovett declined them all, but did agree to informally advise the president as the need arose. Their motto might well have been that of Groton Preparatory School: *Cui servire est regnare*: "To serve is to rule."

Later, when America became increasingly stuck to the Vietnam tar baby, the legacy of the Wise Men was questioned, even within the confines of the Establishment itself. Washington insiders would pejoratively refer to these individuals as the "Wise Men" after Lyndon Johnson called upon them to advise him on the conduct of the war. Johnson hoped that, because they really didn't understand the nature of the country's involvement in Southeast Asia, they would tell him precisely what he wanted to hear.

Perhaps their legacy was a mixed one. But in light of Iranamok, in which key foreign policy officials intentionally distanced themselves from the policy to protect their personal reputations, this fascinating book shows that the "Wise Men's" relative selflessness and professionalism must be viewed with some wistfulness.

The Detroit News, March 11, 1987

A Novel Plan for Post-Apartheid South Africa

(After Apartheid: The Solution for South Africa by Frances Kendall and Leon Louw; Institute for Contemporary Studies Press [1987])

Most books on South Africa concentrate on criticizing that country's government-sponsored racism. But, *After Apartheid: The Solution for South Africa* goes beyond this universally shared condemnation, offering a sedate and compelling plan for peaceful, post-apartheid government. The novel approach of this book, a best-seller in South Africa that is now available in the United States, has thus drawn endorsements ranging from Winnie Mandela, wife of jailed black nationalist leader Nelson Mandela, to members of the ruling Afrikaner establishment.

Authors Frances Kendall and Leon Louw, who are wife and husband, present many historical insights that counter current assumptions. One myth is that South African apartheid was an invention of the conservative National Party, which came to power in 1948. Kendall and Louw note that apartheid actually began in 1660, when newly arrived white settlers promptly barred yellow-skinned natives from 6,000 acres of their own grazing land by planting a boundary of trees.

The fact that apartheid is deeply rooted in the country's culture is one reason why it cannot be eradicated simply by pressuring American companies to "disinvest." As the authors point out several times, the South African people must generate positive changes.

Indeed, black majority rule in South Africa need not necessarily result in a Marxist government, as has been the case in other parts of Africa. *After Apartheid* points out that long before European settlers arrived in the area now comprising South Africa, native tribes had adopted a sophisticated system of government that respected both private property and free enterprise.

Tribal blacks, who were primarily small entrepreneurs and farmers, flourished, as did the economy of the region. As early as the 1870s, the purchasing power of blacks in the eastern cape area exceeded $4.5 million a year.

This economic success engendered much jealousy from the competing Europeans. Kendall and Louw write that "not only were blacks better farmers but they were also competing with white farm-ers for land." This jealousy was compounded by blacks' economic self-sufficiency, which meant they were unavailable to work on white farms or in the gold mines where labor was in short supply. "As a result," the authors say, "a series of laws were passed which robbed blacks of almost all economic freedom."

Among the early colonial government's laws was one designed to force blacks into the labor market by limiting their ability to make a living as farmers. For example, black ownership of land was restricted to 10 acres per farmer, an insufficient amount for a farmer to support his family. The limitation also dampened any incentive for blacks to excel at that occupation.

The reader may be surprised to learn that the colonial govern-ment openly admitted that it was trying to prevent black economic competition and political aspirations. In this sense, the colonial gov-ernment was far more intellectually honest about the nature and pur-pose of apartheid than the current party has ever been. For while the National Party did not invent apartheid, it did invent the ridiculous notion that apartheid was instituted to benefit South African blacks as well as whites.

So, the authors find that the blacks' ability to govern compe-tently is not the issue in making the transition to a post-apartheid government. Other "black African countries are not impoverished because blacks run them, but because their economic policies are wrong. Most black South Africans are not frustrated simply because whites rule them, but because they suffer under bureaucracy, red tape, over-regulation, and mettlesome officialdom. The real problem is not the color of the people who control the machine, but the nature of the machine."

That machine is not a bastion of free-market liberalism, but a regulation of everything from the price of candy bars to the number of sheets contained on a roll of toilet paper. Consequently, the authors consider the Afrikaner's pervasive government regulation a form of "hidden apartheid" that impoverishes whites as well as blacks.

The great task with which the authors struggle is how to fashion a post-apartheid government that ensures for all South African citizens the rights currently enjoyed by only the few. The current government understandably is reluctant to hand over the reins of power, considering how it has treated the black majority. So Kendall and Louw propose a series of essentially autonomous local governmental units fashioned after the Swiss canton system. Each of the cantons—the authors propose about 306 of them—would determine its own political philosophy, governing body, and policies on such matters as education and the economy.

A bicameral central government would be limited to matters of general concern such as national defense and foreign affairs. Each canton would enjoy proportional representation in the central government. Because blacks currently constitute the vast majority of the country, both the central government and most cantons would likely have black majorities.

It is interesting to note the proposed plan would not necessarily eliminate racial discrimination. Private parties—including employers—would be free to integrate or segregate voluntarily. The difference is that all levels of government would be prohibited from practicing racial discrimination. The authors apparently believe the resulting economic competition between the cantons would ultimately make racial discrimination unprofitable.

While the canton system appears enticing, one immediate concern is the possible emergence of several wealthy, white cantons and a lot of poor black ones. After all, the mineral and industrial wealth of

South Africa is not evenly distributed across the country's geography. Kendall and Louw are aware of this potential drawback, but they say the presence of black majorities in most cantons and the constitutionally protected freedoms of all South Africans to move from one canton to another would prevent the current ruling class from dominating the economically rich areas of the country.

Although *After Apartheid's* proposed solution is by no means perfect, it nevertheless presents a thoughtful alternative to the violence now sweeping that country. At the least, it's a good starting point for discussing how to end both the bloodshed and a morally indefensible system.

The Detroit News, July 8, 1987

Black Leadership in American Society

(*Plural but Equal: Blacks and Minorities in America's Plural Society* by Harold Cruse; Morrow [1987])

This thought-provoking book, *Plural but Equal*, examines the role of minorities, particularly blacks, in contemporary American society. It has created some controversy because it criticizes the so-called black leadership.

One of the book's themes is that America is not simply a nation of black and white. Rather, America is made up of a multiplicity of ethnic groups, of which blacks are but one category. This insight has important implications. Unfortunately, the reader may not get this far, for this book is not written for the faint of heart.

The book is written in a wordy style that borders on the ponderous. For example, author Harold Cruse at one point refers to the 1954 *Brown* desegregation decision by saying, "But the constitutional reinterpretation of the sociological evolution of race differences in the body politic prompted the introduction of ethnicity and gender into the civil rights fray in such fashion as graphically to qualify the intent and thrust for the full integration ideals of the NAACP and its supporting civil rights trend."

It is not clear precisely what thought is hidden within that group of words masquerading as a sentence. Perhaps the answer lies in the fact the author is a professor of Afro-American studies at the University of Michigan. The institution's approach to learning was once described as an archeological expedition: students should be willing to dig to find meaning.

The lack of a table of contents also makes it difficult for the reader to follow logically the development of the author's argument. Perhaps Cruse was vaguely aware the book is difficult to navigate because numerous passages are italicized, as if to suggest they would otherwise escape the reader's attention.

That the book's style makes for slow reading is unfortunate because Cruse makes some interesting points. "In America there are minorities, but then there are other minorities; some minorities are equal, but some are more or less equal than others," he writes. "American descendants of European immigrant groups make up what are called 'white ethnics,' who are in fact minorities."

The fact that America is composed of many ethnic groups is important to the book's thesis because blacks then emerge, in a numerical sense, as the largest American ethnic group. Thus, the author reasons that blacks have had the potential to fundamentally influence American society, both politically and economically. He suggests this influence has been squandered, however, in large part due to the traditional focus of the civil rights movement.

Cruse's treatment of the early civil rights movement—which he correctly notes began not in the 1960s but in the latter half of the 19th century—is both informative and fascinating. It reminds us that our nation's history did not begin with our generation, but is part of a continuum. What is also interesting is the conclusion that the traditional civil rights movement placed too much reliance on integration and legal remedies to achieve civil rights for blacks and not enough emphasis on the importance of self-reliance, particularly economic self-reliance.

Cruse notes that early civil rights organizations such as the National Association for the Advancement of Colored People (NAACP) were led by what he calls noneconomic liberals. When the NAACP was founded in the early part of this century, its leadership "split over the primacy of economic questions over civil rights questions or vice versa. Unable to resolve this conflict programmatically at the time of its founding, the NAACP dispensed with an economic program and projected a purely civil rights, or as it was then perceived, a 'civil libertarian' program."

It seems the civil rights movement was premised on the mistaken notion that the ills suffered by blacks could be redressed primarily through the legal process. Civil rights leaders, and the Democratic Party of which they became clients, relied on the federal judiciary to expand the range of rights found in the Constitution. Over time, civil rights activists have been joined by a host of other clients such as organized labor, women's and gay rights groups and so forth with which the party is now synonymous. One need only recall the recent treatment of Robert Bork to understand the extent to which these groups still rely chiefly on the courts to remedy every shortcoming of society.

Legal remedies, even in the hands of an activist judiciary, have their limits, however, as the civil rights movement discovered. The equal protection clause of the 14th Amendment, which was often relied on as the source for equality of civil rights, could not be stretched so far as to require equality of economic rights. Disillusionment resulted in the late 1960s when legal remedies had essentially been exhausted, but discrimination and inequality remained. Having pushed civil rights to its outer social limits, Cruse writes, the Democratic Party had nothing else to offer blacks but good will and some moral support in memory of Martin Luther King.

So what does the author suggest as an alternative? In his view, the demise of the civil rights movement, which he believes began with the 1980s, points to black political organization as the alternative. If by political organization he means blacks should be more active in the political process, then it would be a point with which no one could quarrel. After all, a democracy depends on all of its citizens taking an interest in the affairs of government. Unfortunately, the author flirts with the idea of an independent, black political party.

Even if one ignores the considerable, practical difficulty of starting an independent party, the notion of starting one for blacks is no answer. It implicitly assumes blacks are of one mind on important matters of the day. Thus the term "black leader" is often tossed around as if the individual it describes has the authority to speak for others who may in fact have nothing in common but skin color. Black Americans no more think alike than we all look alike. Ultimately, America is not only a society of ethnics, but one of individuals as well.

The Detroit News, November 25, 1987

Jackson: Motivation and the Message

(*Straight from the Heart* by Jesse Jackson;
Fortress Press [1987])

In his keynote address at the 1984 Democratic convention, Jesse Jackson allowed as how God was not yet done with him. If the presidential race thus far is any indication, Jackson may have been right. The nomination process is more than half complete and Jackson has apparently already exceeded the number of delegates he won in 1984.

Consequently, many members of the media keep asking, "What does Jackson want?" Not only is there something patronizing in the question (for example, no one asks what Mike Dukakis and Al Gore want), but it is the wrong question. The implicit assumption is that since Jackson can't win, he must be after something else. Thus the media has largely ignored the substance of his campaign and has not subjected his public policy stands to proper scrutiny. The correct question is whether Jesse Jackson—regardless of color—has the requisite experience and correct policy proposals to be the Democratic Party's nominee and perhaps the next president.

A recent collection of Jackson's speeches, compiled in a book titled *Straight from the Heart*, supplies some answers. Even in print, Jackson's oratorical style stands out, although it is not easy to define. William F. Buckley has described it as "anaphoric," the rhetorical repetition of the initial phrase of a sentence. Someone else has said Jackson is one of few public figures who can give a speech in iambic pentameter. There are occasions, however, when his penchant for alliteration exceeds even the boundaries of his unique style.

For example, Jackson says in one of his speeches that "it is not your aptitude, but your attitude, that will determine your altitude, with a little intestinal fortitude." Give me a break.

While the book reinforces Jackson's image as a powerful public speaker, what the reader should focus on is the content. In seeking the presidency, Jackson swims against the historical tide, not only because of his color, but because of his lack of elective experience. Only two men in this century—Herbert Hoover and Dwight Eisenhower—became president without prior electoral experience. Because Jackson has never held elected office, the reader must rely on the speeches to discern what type of president Jackson would be.

While the book is organized into sections—Jackson's role as "Political Progressive" or "Preacher" or "Corporate and Cultural Critic"—most of the speeches deal with the same theme. That is blacks must not be taken for granted. He notes at one point that if blacks "follow the strategy of blindly giving our vote to one political faction, we will have power but no leverage."

But has Jackson practiced what he has preached (no pun intended)? Some commentators would argue that by advocating an active big government as the surest path to a just society, he has encouraged blacks to cast their lot exclusively with liberal Democrats. If so, the collective abandonment by blacks of the two-party system may explain why the Democratic Party can afford to take blacks for granted, as it has often been accused of doing.

Jackson has concentrated on economic policies this year, and this subject is also dealt with in the book. Even though Jackson's speeches often extol the virtues of economic self-sufficiency, he can't quite seem to accept the possibility that some ideas advocated by Republicans—such as lower taxes and less government—might help achieve it.

For example, his speeches continually criticize the Reagan administration for being hostile to minority interests, while failing to note that median income for blacks has risen substantially between 1981 and 1986; it fell during the Carter administration.

The book does provide insights into what some of Jackson's priorities might be. Education is one of them. His Chicago-based

Operation PUSH has done much to promote the value of education. For example, it has provided many high school students with information on financial resources for college.

His efforts to end drug abuse have been commendable. The same is true with respect to his efforts to extend the franchise to citizens who have not traditionally voted. He correctly notes that living in a democracy entails not only rights but responsibilities, one of the most important of which is taking an abiding interest in selecting those who govern us. In another instance, during a tortured analysis of California's Proposition 13, Jackson offers a perceptive view that the property tax is an antiquated way to finance primary education and contributes to inequality.

The same cannot be said of his positions on other issues. On the role of nuclear weapons, for example, his statement that "we must choose the human race over the nuclear race" is about as profound as Paul Simon's notion that foreign policy should be based on caring about people. It oversimplifies a complex aspect of the world we live in. While one may wish that nuclear weapons did not exist, it cannot be ignored that nuclear deterrence has played an important role in maintaining peace during the postwar era. When was the last time European countries were at peace with each other for 43 consecutive years?

Unfortunately, the book doesn't deal with many of the issues Jackson has raised recently, because the book only covers his speeches through early 1986. Thus, there are no specifics about his plan to use workers' pension funds for economic "reinvestment"; no explanation of how his plan to negotiate directly with the Palestinian Liberation Organization would affect prospects in the Middle East; no analysis of how his plan to repeal the Reagan tax cuts would affect the economy.

These proposals may be worthwhile or they may be loony, but one thing is certain: They deserve the same degree of scrutiny that would be accorded if advanced by any other candidate. Only then can voters make an informed decision.

The Detroit News, March 23, 1988

Bush Ought to Be "Thinking about America"

(Thinking About America: The United States in the 1990s, Edited by Annelise Anderson and Dennis Bark; Hoover Institution Press [1988])

With the Cabinet selections complete and the inauguration only a couple days away, President-elect George Bush no doubt has given considerable thought to how best to govern the country. *Thinking About America: The United States in the 1990s* offers a compelling view of what the Bush administration and Americans ought to concentrate on.

The book, which was published by the Hoover Institution at Stanford University, consists of 47 essays dealing with foreign policy and national security, international economic policy, domestic affairs and governmental philosophy. Among the essayists are three former presidents, soon-to-be former President Reagan, four Nobel-Prize recipients, and assorted other luminaries.

The Hoover Institution published a similar book in 1980 that became a blueprint for Reagan administration policy. One can only hope *Thinking About America* has a similar influence on the Bush administration.

A large number of essays concentrate on U.S.-Soviet relations, with several of them casting doubt on the Soviet Union's newly professed friendliness. Henry Rowen, former president of Rand Corporation, and John Dunlop, a senior fellow at Hoover, contend the Soviet Union does not wish to change its behavior, but is being forced to by economic conditions beyond its control. They advise that to the extent the United States alleviates these conditions, it also removes any incentive for the Soviets to institute meaningful change.

Indeed, Mikhail Gorbachev may not be the new breed of Soviet leader portrayed by the media. Richard Starr, a senior fellow at Hoover, notes that from 1978 through 1987, Soviet military expenditures were two-thirds higher than America's and produced nine times as many artillery pieces, five times as many surface-to-air missiles, more than three times as many tanks, and twice the number of fighters, helicopters, and submarines.

In fact, there are striking similarities between Gorbachev's programs and those pursued by Nikita Khrushchev in the 1950s. Gorbachev may simply be another Khrushchev, made more palatable to Western tastes by virtue of a better tailor and slimmer wife.

What clearly does interest the Soviet Union is Western technology, which it has been unable to produce for itself, and greater access to Western financial assistance. For example, Roger Robinson, Jr., formerly with the National Security Council, points out that the Soviet Union and Eastern Bloc countries borrowed $24 billion from the west in 1986, most of it in general purpose loans with no restrictions on how it could be spent.

Thus, the West is potentially helping to finance Soviet adventurism and perhaps even terrorist activity by Soviet client states such as Syria and Libya. Robinson suggests this potential self-inflicted threat to Western security could be greatly reduced if Western banks would adopt more prudent lending practices.

Closer to home is Latin and Central America. Robert Wesson, a Hoover expert on Soviet and Latin American affairs, notes that while the Reagan Administration has been concerned primarily with communist insurgency in Nicaragua and El Salvador, the region struggles under a $400-billion foreign debt and economic depression. American protectionism has made it difficult for these countries to improve the balance of payments by exporting legitimate products and has made marijuana and cocaine the region's major cash exports.

Wesson proposes removing trade barriers and restructuring existing debt to permit an influx of capital. Economist Melvyn

Krauss also calls for removing trade barriers so Third World countries can have access to American markets. Using market-place economics—America's strongest institution—would be a more effective method of combating the spread of communism, Krauss argues, than foreign aid.

These essays reinforce a recurring theme in the book: that America, as the exemplar of Western tradition, must continue to play a pre-eminent role in world affairs. Thus, editor Dennis Bark recommends strengthening U.S. relations with Western Europe based on our common traditions and values. In doing so, he rejects the view of those, at home and abroad, who belittle the values and achievements of Western civilization by labeling it as racist, sexist, and imperialistic.

An example of such belittlement, interestingly enough, was Stanford's decision last year to include female and minority authors to its course on Western civilization—not because of the merit of the books, but in answer to complaints that the classic works studied were all written by "dead white men."

The subject of balancing the federal budget has dominated the media since the election, and political scientist Aaron Wildavsky of the University of California at Berkeley offers an insightful view of why it won't be an easy task. The inability to balance the budget can't be blamed so much on process, according to Wildavsky, as on a fundamental disagreement over the role of government.

Liberal Democrats are motivated by a desire to do good deeds (with other people's money) while Republicans are motivated by a desire to limit government as the best means of allowing taxpayers to spend their own money. Wildavsky also notes that the Reagan tax cuts, blamed by many analysts as causing the deficit, merely reduced the percentage of gross national product taken by federal taxes to the level traditionally in effect before Jimmy Carter took office.

Atlanta Mayor Andrew Young offers a thoughtful analysis of the challenges facing American cities such as Detroit. Since cities, in Young's view, are free markets of politics, he argues that these challenges should be treated as unique opportunities to experiment with new problem-solving techniques.

Young calls for more regional cooperation between inner cities and suburban areas, noting that problems such as crime and poverty do not respect arbitrary governmental boundaries. He also examines the importance of public-private partnerships and recommends the prudent use of privatization as one means of solving the dilemma of financing public improvements and services without increasing taxes.

In contrast to much of last year's presidential campaign, *Thinking About America* provides a practical and thoughtful framework for addressing the public policy issues confronting the country. The contribution made by this work should benefit ordinary citizens who help elect and shape the government, as well as those chosen to lead it.

The Detroit News, January 18, 1989

Cutting the Court's Hold
on Regulation

*(Judicial Compulsions: How Public Law Distorts
Public Policy* by Jeremy Rabkin; Basic Books [1989])

When William F. Buckley was once asked why he had used the obscure word irenic when it meant the same as peaceful, he responded that he desired the additional syllable. Apparently when writing *Judicial Compulsions*, author Jeremy Rabkin, a professor of government at Cornell University, was not content with an additional syllable or two. The author's lack of lucidity is unfortunate because it tends to distract the reader from the important point he attempts to make, a point that could have been developed quite adequately without references to the law of Moses, the philosophies of Kant, or aspects of non-Euclidean geometry.

The book analyzes what the author sees as the unfortunate and increasing tendency of federal courts to intervene, or to permit advocacy groups to intervene, into the policymaking affairs of federal regulatory agencies. Rabkin's criticism is not simply that courts lack the capacity to manage executive branch functions, but also that regulatory agencies are obligated to serve the public at large rather than special interests. Therefore, private and unaccountable advocacy groups should not be permitted to exert undue influence on public policy.

In Rabkin's opinion, the traditional purpose of courts is to uphold private "rights," not to manage social "interests." Federal judges, he believes, have confused these two concepts. Rabkin notes that rights, such as the right to property or of contract, belong to individuals rather than to groups. Therefore, only a person possessing a right that is allegedly violated may seek redress in the courts. Thus, he notes that in deference to the traditional view, a suit by an environmental advocacy group, for example, demanding more vigorous regulatory action may be described as an effort to enforce a "right" to clean air or a "right" to some other regulatory benefit.

But claims to regulatory benefits differ from conventional legal rights in several important respects. First, regulatory disputes are usually much more complex and confusing because they are disputes about general policy goals, the achievement of which may permit regulatory agencies to exercise discretion. The nature of some policy goals may make it difficult to identify who is harmed should the policy not be achieved. For example, it would be difficult for an individual to show that the nation's acid rain policy resulted in harm that differed from that affecting other citizens.

Second, the lack of an appropriate plaintiff, one who can allege a personal injury, makes it difficult for a court to determine what judicial relief to grant. Allowing third parties to insist on pursuing the legal rights of others means that those rights no longer remain under the control of individuals who possess them.

Rabkin argues that this is precisely what happens when federal courts permit special interest groups to sue regulatory agencies on behalf of the "public interest." When a business firm asserts its rights in court, it can be assumed to speak for the owners. "However, when an advocacy group comes to court to assert the right to clean air or to enforce some equally general policy goal," he writes, "it asserts a claim to something over which it does not have exclusive control." And by what authority, Rabkin asks, does a private advocacy group presume to speak for the public at large?

The author documents how special interest groups use the leverage gained by litigation, or the threat of litigation, to bargain with regulatory agencies about public policy. One result is that executive branch agencies, which are supposed to be accountable through the president to the public, become accountable instead to self-appointed and unelected guardians of the public interest, as these groups see it.

Judicial intervention also saps time and resources that might have been better used to achieve public policy benefits.

In 1970, for example, the NAACP's Legal Defense Fund filed suit on behalf of a black student who attended a segregated school in Mississippi. The allegation was that since the school district was segregated, it should no longer receive federal funds.

But, instead of suing the local school authorities, as civil rights lawyers had been doing for years in similar cases, including the landmark *Brown* decision, the defense fund sued the federal office of civil rights. It alleged a pattern of inaction regarding desegregation efforts in 17 Southern and border states.

The result was a protracted lawsuit. For more than a decade, the agency and the NAACP defense fund wrangled over statistics and compliance deadlines relating to racial balance—as though racial balance within each school was the end in itself.

The lawsuit produced two ironies. First, not only the federal office of civil rights, but also the Legal Defense Fund, became so absorbed in the lawsuit that both apparently lost sight of what the real goal should have been: improving educational opportunities for minority students. But, as the author notes, the academic performance of black students actually declined throughout the lawsuit. The second irony was that after more than a decade of judicial intervention into the affairs of the civil rights agency, the presiding federal judge dismissed the suit on grounds that the plaintiffs lacked standing.

Advocacy groups' influence on public policy through litigation can reinforce bureaucratic inertia by causing regulatory agencies to be overly cautious. Regulatory agencies may be unwilling to undertake new beneficial policy initiatives out of fear of being sued.

Judicial Compulsions deserves thoughtful consideration, despite Rabkin's inability to convey why the important problem of judicial intervention should concern not just students of government, but citizens as well.

The Detroit News, December 27, 1989

Will South Africa Embrace Free-Market System?

(*South Africa's War against Capitalism* by Walter Williams; a Cato Institute Book [1989])

The South African government recently freed black activist Nelson Mandela, who was imprisoned nearly three decades ago, and lifted its ban on the African National Congress. These are hopeful signs that South Africa is not entirely immune to winds of freedom now sweeping Eastern Europe. But, whether South Africa will embrace free markets and capitalism as it turns away from apartheid remains to be seen.

Several years ago, Archbishop Desmond Tutu declared himself to be opposed to capitalism. In a similar vein, Winnie Mandela indicated the Soviet Union represented the model to which a post-apartheid South Africa should aspire. The irony is that the Soviet Union apparently is no longer a model even for itself.

One can only hope Winnie Mandela has changed her mind. Otherwise her views, as well as Tutu's, are troubling because they suggest South Africa is a capitalist nation and that apartheid is the result of capitalistic excesses. In his new book, *South Africa's War Against Capitalism*, George Mason University economics professor Walter Williams makes the case that the opposite is true. Williams, who happens to be black, argues that the whole ugly history of apartheid has been an attack on free markets and individual rights as well as a glorification of centralized governmental power.

So much has been written about the legally sanctioned racism which is at the core of apartheid that it may be surprising to learn that South African common law accords each person the same basic freedoms and individual rights, regardless of race. But there is one important distinction between individual rights as most Americans understand them and as they exist in South Africa. In this country, the Constitution, particularly the Bill of Rights, protects citizens from the capricious acts of the government, while the South African constitution provides few safeguards that the legislative branch cannot supersede.

The will of the South African parliament is absolute and the role of the courts is merely to enforce that will. Few areas of human activity are immune to legislative regulation. For example, parliament has passed laws requiring the classification of its citizens by race, prohibiting mixed marriages, restricting by race where persons may live and under what circumstances, and requiring separate facilities for different races.

But Williams' main focus is legislative regulation of race in the South African labor market. A variety of laws require certain jobs be held by whites only. The necessity for such restrictions is not readily apparent because whites own and manage most so-regulated industries. Thus, Williams notes that "if racism were the complete answer, racial laws would be unnecessary because white business owners and government agencies simply would not hire blacks for jobs which were desirable to whites." The mere existence of the laws suggests white business owners would otherwise hire blacks.

The author contends special interest groups have used the unrestricted power of the South African parliament to enact such laws in order to protect themselves from the competition inherent in the marketplace. For example, when whites were unable to compete with black farmers, they legislatively limited the acreage that black farmers could own. One result was that many blacks who could no longer make a living as farmers sought work in urban areas. Such restrictions also benefited white mine owners, who had been unable to obtain workers as long as blacks were self-sufficient.

Economically speaking, any government policy, including legalized discrimination, that is designed to create special privileges for one group, also tends to produce corresponding disadvantages for some other group. South Africa has proved to be no exception.

Though mostly non-white South Africans have borne those disadvantages, members of the white population have also suffered economically. Many white teachers are unemployed due to declining enrollments among white students, while there is a simultaneous shortage of teachers in many black townships. This has led to resistance, even evasion and contravention of racially discriminatory laws, even by persons who share the same white supremacist ideology as the government officials and politicians who enacted the apartheid laws.

In essence, many white South Africans have found their racial views to be at odds with their pocketbooks. Williams cites instances of white union leaders calling for laws requiring mine owners to pay black workers the same wages as their white counterparts. To the naïve, such calls might be seen as an improvement in South African attitudes toward blacks. But, in fact, labor leaders have recognized that higher wages won by white unions have placed their members at a competitive disadvantage, thereby increasing the attractiveness of cheaper black workers.

Williams concludes with a cautionary note, suggesting that even if official apartheid is eliminated, its victims must remain vigilant lest it re-emerge as what he terms "apartheid in camouflage."

"Apartheid is a special case of the kinds of restrictions that are achieved when one class of individuals acquire privileges through the use of state violence to deny another class of individuals the right to engage in voluntary and mutually agreeable exchanges," he writes. Apartheid in camouflage, Williams warns, could take the form of occupational licensing laws requiring government sanction of individuals to carry on certain trades, or placing numerical limits on the number of persons in certain trades or regulating minimum and maximum prices.

It is not clear how the drama presently unfolding in South Africa will play out. Although the Western media typically portray the situation as a struggle pitting the black majority against the white minority, the problems South Africans face are far more complex.

For starters, the black population consists of several distinct ethnic groups, each with different customs, values, and even languages. When people casually use the phrase "the blacks of South Africa," it has about as much precision as the "whites of Europe." Or the whites of South Africa, for that matter.

Walter Williams' *South Africa's War Against Capitalism* presents a persuasive argument for free-market capitalism in a post-apartheid South Africa. If Winnie Mandela remains unconvinced, she should place a call to Mikhail Gorbachev.

The Detroit News, February 14, 1990

Judicial Intervention Has Mixed Track Record

(Courts, Corrections, and the Constitution, Edited by John J. Dilulio, Jr.; Oxford University Press [1991])

In Federalist No. 78, Alexander Hamilton observed that of the three branches of government, the judiciary was least dangerous to the rights of the people because it had no influence over either the sword or the purse. It was generally accepted in Hamilton's day that courts were to fulfill the limited role of declaring what the law was in the context of particular legal disputes.

Times have changed. While today's courts may not comprise the most dangerous of the three branches of government, their influence is certainly no longer, to use Montesquieu's words, "next to nothing." One area in which the judicial influence has been most keenly felt is in the operations of jails and prisons. During the past 30 years, state and federal courts have become one of the chief agents of change in this nation's penal institutions. It is an understatement to say that much of the change which has been wrought by courts in this area has not been without considerable controversy.

Courts, Corrections, and the Constitution, edited by John J. Dilulio, Jr., of Princeton University, chronicles in a series of thoughtful and thought-provoking essays the mixed judicial record. The book examines some of the more celebrated examples of judicial intervention in correctional matters, such as the *Ruiz* case that was initiated in federal district court in 1972 by an inmate in the Texas state prison system, and the *Guthrie* case, filed the same year

29

as *Ruiz*, that brought about sweeping changes in the Georgia correctional system.

This book is particularly relevant to Michigan since several governmental units in this state have had extensive experience with inmate lawsuits. Two years ago, for example, Wayne County Circuit Court removed control of the county jail from the sheriff and appointed the county executive as receiver as part of an ongoing class action lawsuit that was filed by inmates in 1971. Also, a number of this state's prisons have been operating under federal court supervision for some years. In one instance the state has been paying a $1,000 a day fine since last fall—recently increased to $10,000 a day—for failure to comply with a federal consent decree.

The essays that comprise the book exemplify two broad schools of thought about the role courts should play. At one end of the spectrum is what may be referred to as the traditional view, which holds that the distinctive competence of courts lies in their ability to resolve disputes according to an established set of legal rules. According to this perspective, it is appropriate for judges to hear inmate lawsuits and to impose remedies when constitutional violations are found, but inappropriate for judges to attempt to run penal institutions, since they possess no particular expertise as managers or administrators. Therefore, courts overreach not only their authority, but also their competence when they attempt to micro-manage correctional policy.

The other perspective is that courts, particularly federal courts, should act as agents for social change by giving meaning and content to underlying constitutional values as they affect public institutions. Courts should not only redress past injuries, but prevent future ones by restructuring bureaucratic institutions like prisons and jails. According to this perspective, judges should not limit themselves to traditional judicial authority, but should feel free to wield powers that are more commonly associated with the legislative and executive branches of government. For example, a judge should feel free to act as an administrator to redirect public resources (read tax dollars) for the benefit of deprived segments of society. In short, judges should be social reformers.

The real question separating the two perspectives is not whether courts have a role to play in the area of corrections, but rather what that role should be. On balance, those essayists who contend for a more limited, traditional role for courts make the better case. Not only do judges lack any special claim to expertise in the subject matter of correctional policy, but as the book points out, despite the numerous inmate lawsuits that have been heard and court orders that have been issued, there is no empirical evidence to show whether the results have actually changed prisons for the better.

Furthermore, judges tend to be far more unaccountable to the public for their actions than are their legislative and executive branch counterparts. This is certainly true of federal judges, who are appointed for life. The insulation from public opinion that judges generally enjoy is perfectly appropriate so long as their role is properly limited to deciding what the law is, but far less justifiable when judges become nothing more than policymakers who happen to wear black robes. (For example, Michigan courts have had to hear several lawsuits aimed at blocking state budget cuts, some of which have already been signed into law, even though the real crux of the lawsuits had more to do with policy differences over what programs should be funded than with questions of law.)

The rule which should guide judicial activity in the corrections areas is that which should guide judicial activity in general: common sense. In other words, a judicial remedy should be narrowly tailored to suit that violation. For example, there is a tremendous difference between a court order upholding an inmate's right to appeal his or her conviction and a court order decreeing the number and type of books that must be acquired for the prison law library; or between an order upholding an inmate's right to decent food and one decreeing the precise temperature at which a meal must be served. All too often inmate lawsuits have resulted in sweeping orders that went far beyond correcting the grievance originally at issue.

The writers who contributed to *Courts, Corrections, and the Constitution* would seem to agree that courts will continue to play an important role in shaping correctional institutions. This book offers a compelling view of a number of issues that should guide that involvement.

The Detroit News, April 10, 1991

Civil Rights Issues More Divisive Than Ever

(*Civil Rights Under Reagan* by Robert Detlefsen;
Institute for Contemporary Studies Press [1991])

A generation ago, this country celebrated the passage of the 1964 Civil Rights Act. It was a testament to the principle that all Americans should be judged on the basis of merit rather than skin color.

Fast forward to 1991. The country is in the midst of a divisive civil rights debate that has been anything but civil. Even before the recent nomination of Clarence Thomas to the U.S. Supreme Court and debate over new civil rights legislation, many Americans had an uneasy feeling that the civil rights train had gotten off track. What went wrong?

Civil Rights Under Reagan attempts to supply some answers. Robert Detlefsen, who teaches political science at the University of California at Berkeley, tells how many civil rights laws that were enacted to end discrimination have actually been used to justify reverse discrimination. In fact, in 1984, two members of the U.S. Civil rights Commission issued a statement asserting that the civil rights laws were not intended to protect white males from discrimination.

Ronald Reagan entered office in 1981 vowing to end preferential treatment. However, as the author observes, the Reagan administration had surprisingly little success at redirecting civil rights policy toward its original goal of equal opportunity for individuals without regard to race or gender. To the contrary, the view of affirmative action as quotas was so entrenched that the Reagan administration was castigated by the civil rights establishment for advocating a color-blind interpretation of the Constitution.

One of the most extraordinary themes that emerges from the book is that Congress, the nation's policymaking body, has played virtually no part in developing civil rights policies during the past two decades. These policies have been developed chiefly by two of the most unaccountable parts of the federal government: federal courts and executive agency bureaucrats. This may explain why these issues remain so divisive.

It didn't have to be this way. The book recounts the history of civil rights legislation passed in the early 1960s, correctly noting it was intended to promote equality of opportunity by securing equality before the law. For example, when affirmative action was first mentioned in a 1961 presidential executive order, the term meant only that employers should publicize job vacancies and encourage applications from minorities who might otherwise not apply because of past discrimination. Now, to many, affirmative action is synonymous with reverse discrimination and quotas.

It was hoped that the early civil rights measures ensuring equality of opportunity would eventually bring about equality of condition. "But," as Detlefsen points out, "almost as soon as this original sequence was codified into law and public policy, legal and political activists began to reverse this sequence to make equality of condition the objective."

A major turning point came in 1971 when the U.S. Supreme Court decided *Griggs* vs. *Duke Power Company*. At issue was the company's requirement that all job applicants take a standardized test and possess a high school diploma.

The court held that such neutral employment criteria were presumptively illegal under the Civil Rights Act if they produced a "disparate impact" adverse to minorities. Because blacks as a group did not perform as well on the test and were less likely to have a high school diploma, the employer bore the burden of proving these employment criteria were job-related. The fact that an employer might prefer high school graduates because it found them to be better, more highly-motivated employees was irrelevant.

The *Griggs* decision was significant for two reasons. First, it regrettably gave judicial approval to dismantling the historical practice, backed by statutes and the Constitution, of applying equitable relief to specific individuals who alleged a violation of specific rights. "Today all this has changed," Detlefsen writes, "but perhaps the most momentous change concerns the frequent substitution of broad social groups (usually defined by racial and gender criteria where civil rights violations are alleged) for specific individuals in fashioning equitable relief."

Second, statistical proof of alleged discrimination became more important than proof of actual discrimination. "Because disparate impact renders the issue of discriminatory purpose or intent irrelevant," the author notes, "statistical evidence necessarily became the sole basis for advancing and rebutting allegations of unlawful discrimination."

Furthermore, even though *Griggs* dealt only with standardized tests and high school diplomas, it did not take lower federal courts long to expand the range of hiring criteria that employers could not use. On occasion, the results were absurd. For example, one court held that employers could not refuse to hire applicants with multiple arrest records because national statistics showed that blacks, as a group, were arrested more often than whites.

These kinds of decisions naturally upset people. Democrats already concede that hiring quotas are a cutting issue for Republicans. This fact may explain why Congress in the past has not aggressively pursued civil rights legislation. Preferential treatment might never be enacted if it actually had to be put to a vote.

As it turns out, Detlefsen notes, Reagan's influence on civil rights has increased since he left office. His appointees to the Supreme Court have helped to overturn prior civil rights rulings. That's why the confirmation hearings of Clarence Thomas are so important. They have become an alternative forum for America to work out its feelings on issues such as affirmative action.

Hopefully, *Civil Rights Under Reagan* will contribute to a reasoned debate about these important issues, which the country has been denied for too long.

The Detroit News, September 11, 1991

Setting Realistic Goals in the War on Drugs

(*Against Excess: Drug Policy for Results* by Mark A.R. Kleiman; Basic Books [1991])

Few matters of national public policy are more deserving of serious consideration, yet more prone to simplistic solution, than America's drug problem. Proposed solutions often defy ideological boundaries. Conservative William F. Buckley and libertarian Milton Friedman favor legalization, or at least decriminalization, while liberal Charles Rangel opposes both approaches. What seems clear is that what has been tried has not worked very well.

A new book by Mark Kleiman, *Against Excess: Drug Policy for Results*, makes a persuasive case for adopting a middle course between blanket prohibition and total legalization. Kleiman, a professor at Harvard's Kennedy School of Government and a former Justice Department drug policy analyst, argues that the use of certain drugs should be treated as a new social and legal category of "grudgingly tolerated vices." Under the author's approach, drugs such as alcohol, nicotine, and marijuana would be strictly prohibited only to minors and to adults who had shown an inability to use them responsibly. Such drugs would be available to the remainder of the adult population, but subject to negative advertising, higher levels of taxation than other goods, and promotion restrictions. Demonstrably dangerous drugs, such as crack cocaine, would remain prohibited.

Kleiman's inclusion of alcohol and tobacco among the substances to be addressed by an enlightened national drug policy is a bit unsettling to those of us who occasionally enjoy a good wine during dinner and cigars afterward. This is because, as the author notes, "the legal distinction between licit and illicit drugs is sometimes treated as if it had pharmacological significance. Vendors of licit drugs and proponents of a 'drug-free society' share an interest in convincing tobacco smokers and alcohol drinkers that smoking and drinking are radically different than drug use."

To some extent, however, they are radically different. Cigar smokers don't generally commit crimes to support their "habit" and wine dealers don't kill each other, or innocent bystanders, in gun battles over profits or territory. On the other hand, Kleiman does have a point when he notes the distinction between permitted and prohibited drugs is more conventional and a function of social mores than natural. "The Koran forbids wine, not hashish; the Controlled Substances Act hashish, but not wine; the prohibitions in the Book of Mormon are taken to preclude both, along with nicotine and caffeine."

One of the more fascinating aspects of the book is its description of how drugs, and their users, often exhibit markedly different characteristics from each other. According to Kleiman, a substantial proportion of all heroin users steal or deal drugs to earn money, while the majority of marijuana users engage in neither activity. Heroin and crack are generally sold by professional dealers outdoors or at particular locations, while powder cocaine and marijuana are more likely to change hands indoors.

Similarly, "heroin and crack users tend to buy at most a day's supply at a time; marijuana users often buy for a month or more; cocaine users are in between." One of the major flaws in current drug policy approaches is the tendency to ignore these and other differences. Instead, drug abuse is treated as a single problem "to be addressed by a single set of policies, all designed around the theme of reducing drug consumption."

While arguing for a more enlightened approach to drug policy, Kleiman does say drugs differ from other commodities in ways that justify special attention under our laws. Not only are drugs dangerous because of the physical toll they exact on users and expensive in money and time wasted under their influence; they also tend to distort rational behavior. Most of our social institutions, indeed our basic system of government, is premised upon individual pursuit of enlightened self-interest. As Kleiman points out, "we expect our fellow citizens to be good stewards of their own welfare; under no other assumption does either the market economy or personal liberty make sense as a way of securing good results for individuals or the social group."

Drugs, however, tend to undermine rational behavior through the effects of intoxication, addiction, and distorted perceptions of risk. In short, individuals under the immediate or continued influence of drugs are often not capable of determining what is in the best interest of themselves or others.

As a result, the demand for drugs "does not bear the same relationship to consumers' considered judgments of what is in their own best interest as does the demand for apricots," for example. Thus, Kleiman readily concedes that "it is not at all unreasonable for a society that makes the most of its regulations about consumer choice on the basis of rational actor assumptions to be somewhat more paternalistic when it comes to choices about drug use."

The one drawback to the extremely well-written *Against Excess* is that no sooner does Kleiman advance an idea worthy of consideration then he promptly explains why he is sure the approach will be unlikely to succeed. This minor flaw is excusable because the book raises many important issues. One particularly well-taken point is the suggestion that policymakers should establish realistic goals for dealing with the drug problem. Eradicating all drug use is an admirable goal, but one that is unlikely to be achieved.

It is ironic, Kleiman writes, that addressing drug abuse as a public policy issue has much in common with drug use itself: both are prone to excess and both can cause unwanted side effects. "The problem is to replace excess with moderation in a double sense: a policy to encourage moderation in use and moderation in the implementation of policy."

Against Excess will not fully satisfy legalization advocates or those who want to eradicate the "war on drugs." Given the level of current debate, this may be the best evidence to commend Kleiman's views.

The Detroit News, July 8, 1992

Racial Classifications?
Try the Human Race

(The Racialization of America by
Yehudi O. Webster; St. Martin's Press [1992])

Few subjects are more discussed, but less understood, than the role
of race in American society. Numerous academic works, particularly those dealing with the social sciences, examine the relative
condition of "whites" and "non-whites." In fact, some scholars
claim that race has always been a formative force in American society. But has it?

A recent book by Yehudi Webster, titled *The Racialization of
America*, makes a persuasive argument that it isn't race, or even racism, that has bewildered American society for so long. Instead, it
is the longstanding practice of assigning people to racial categories,
what the author calls "racialization." Webster, a professor of Pan-
African studies at California State University, notes that "racial classification is itself part of a general theory of social relations in which
persons are racially classified and their biological and moral attri-
butes are presented as explanations of their behavior and historical
developments."

The practice of racial classification originated among 18th century natural scientists who were motivated in no small degree by a
desire to find a "scientific" justification for slavery. Prior to that time,
as strange as it may seem, the concept of race was not that significant.

The early settlers of Virginia, for example, did not think of
themselves as white. Surviving legal documents identified them as

"Englishmen" or "Christians." The term "white" developed later as a direct result of slavery. The peculiar institution was an embarrassing contradiction in a country that espoused the importance of religious piety and democratic ideals. However, if slavery could be conceived of as a natural phenomenon by virtue of the natural inferiority of blacks, then slaveholders could be absolved of any wrongdoing.

Interestingly, the practice of racial classification not only survived the institution it was created to justify but, according to the author, continues to thrive in contemporary American society. One reason is that officials at all levels of government implicitly endorse the practice. Racial classifications play prominent roles in governmental estimates of social and demographic conditions.

"On a variety of official documents citizens are requested to state their race or ethnicity," Webster notes. "In census tabulations, they are asked to respond, indeed, confess their races, to examine their skin color, the color of their blood, their type of hair and breadth of their nostrils, to allocate themselves to racial groups." In turn, these arbitrary categories are then often used to explain such things as crime, or poverty, or income disparities.

One irony of the continuing practice of racial classification is that, as Webster points out, there is no general agreement among scientists and anthropologists on how many "races" actually exist. The estimates range anywhere from three to several hundred.

This explains why over time the U.S. Census Bureau has shifted Japanese Americans from categories such as "non-white," "Oriental," or simply "Other" to recent inclusion as a specific ethnic group within the broad category of "Asian and Pacific Islanders." (And, why the term "Hispanic," which is applied to an ever-changing group of U.S. residents, is so amorphous. Hispanic, like "Latino," generally refers to persons whose cultural heritage traces back to a Spanish-speaking country in Latin America, but includes those with links to Spain or from the Southwestern region of the United States that was once under Spanish or Mexican control.)

Another irony of racial classification is that public officials—both liberals and conservatives—and much of the media bemoan the continuing influence of race even while saturating citizens with confused racial categories. This is ironic because citizens are expected not to discriminate on the basis of race, to treat each other as human beings, while at the same time they are forced to see themselves as belong to different groups. This situation is worsened, Webster writes, by "community activists as well as Republican and Democratic party strategists who attempt to capitalize on a racialized social climate generated by academic and official usages of racial classification."

It should come as no surprise then, as Webster notes, that once race is officially endorsed, special interest groups intervene to demand resources for certain races or protection of the position of others. The identification of racial proportions in the population leads inevitably to demands for proportional representation. Racial solutions are developed for what are perceived to be racial problems.

"These solutions, however, generate more problems," Webster says. "Jim Crowism produced the civil rights movement, which called forth affirmative action, black power, and multiculturalism which foster tensions between nonwhites and whites." And so it goes. "In the resulting racial dog-fights citizens cannot see the human forest for the racial trees."

The real tragedy of racial classification is that, by focusing on something as artificial as skin color, it prevents us from achieving color-blind solutions to some of our most difficult problems.

For example, as long as many in the civil rights establishment continue to portray poverty, discrimination, or inadequate education as exclusively "black" afflictions, they should continue to expect an unenthusiastic response from many Americans; not because of racism, but because millions of "whites" also live in poverty and have suffered from exploitation and lack an adequate education.

It needn't be that way.

As the author points out, "Class, or culture, could be the chosen prism through which events are analyzed." In other words, social problems could be classified as human problems.

The Racialization of America is certainly a thought-provoking book. One can only hope it will contribute to a reasoned debate regarding both our relations with one another and the importance of viewing one another as individuals who, in the final analysis, are really part of the same race: the human race.

The Detroit News, December 2, 1992

Addressing the Decline of Shared Values

(The Spirit of Community: Rights, Responsibilities, and the Communitarian Agenda by Amitai Etzioni; Crown [1993])*

The ubiquitous "how to" book has become an increasingly popular part of the culture. Books on practically every endeavor purport to imbue their readers with the skills necessary to achieve some desired result. It is as though all human activity, from losing weight to raising a child, can be reduced to a few easy steps that anyone can master.

It is only natural, then, that there comes a how-to book about improving our citizenship and communities from Amitai Etzioni, a professor at George Washington University and leader of what he refers to as the "communitarian" movement. Despite its sometimes overly exhortatory tone, *The Spirit of Community* addresses a serious topic: the general decline of shared values and sense of community which characterized this nation during much of its history.

A major cause of this decline, as Etzioni sees it, is that we have too many rights. Or more precisely, that there are too many instances in which individuals seek to elevate what are really nothing more than their personal desires into constitutional rights.

Etzioni has a point. Advocates for the homeless contend that affordable housing is a "right." The same is now being said of health-care. The list of rights has grown to become virtually endless. And, unlike privileges, rights do not have to be earned or even paid for by those who wish to enjoy them.

Furthermore, as the author points out, individuals who argue that their claims are based upon rights tend to view those claims as sweeping aside all contrary arguments. Witness the current debate over homosexuals in the military. When the issue is framed, as its advocates want to do, as a gay "rights" issue, genuine debate becomes impossible because anyone who disagrees is accused of depriving individuals of their rights or labeled a homophobe. Etzioni calls for a moratorium on the creation of further new rights because "the incessant issuance of new rights, like the wholesale printing of currency, causes a massive inflation of rights that devalues the moral claim."

Of equal interest are the author's observations about the increasing imbalance between rights and responsibilities. Etzioni notes "a tendency among Americans in recent years to claim rights for themselves and leave responsibilities to the government." For example, although most citizens, if accused of a crime, would consider it their right to be tried by a jury of their peers, few persons display much enthusiasm when called upon to serve on a jury and many go to extraordinary lengths to avoid such responsibility. Etzioni suggests re-establishing the traditional link between such rights and responsibilities.

Etzioni devotes chapters to examining how shared values and a sense of community have been lost and can be restored in institutions such as the family and schools. It is hard to find fault with many of the points advanced by the author; indeed, many of them would have been seen as little more than common sense by earlier generations of Americans.

For example, Etzioni argues that having children is not merely a personal affair, but one that has consequences for the wider community. Parents who are unwilling or unable to properly rear their children inflict the unfortunate results on the entire society. Similarly, Etzioni suggests that schools should do more than merely attempt to transmit skills or knowledge; they should also stress the importance of values, morals, and self-discipline, something that most schools, particularly public schools, are exceedingly reluctant to do.

The book becomes controversial when Etzioni calls for making certain minimum adjustments in individual rights when reasonably required by the public interest. These adjustments would include requiring random drug testing and sobriety check points.

The author anticipates that many critics will not agree. "Radical individualists, such as libertarians and the American Civil Liberties Union have effectively blocked many steps to increase public safety and health." They disagree because they fear that even modest adjustments in the balance between individual rights and social responsibilities would weaken basic liberties.

Yet the author argues that such adjustments can and should be made when there is a clear and present danger to the public safety and health, and no effective alternative exists. Even then, he cautions that the preferred course is to select those options that are the least intrusive.

Therefore, a random drug testing law would target high-risk groups including engineers, airline pilots, and school bus drivers—because of the vast number of lives directly under their control—but not for librarians. Sobriety check points make sense because of the proven danger of driving while intoxicated. But Etzioni argues that they should be done only when announced in advance and conducted efficiently by police. In neither case would it be reasonable to fear such measures as being the first step toward some authoritarian police state.

The Spirit of Community may be greeted with a healthy dose of skepticism. Given that political philosophers since at least the time of Socrates have sought to establish just and virtuous societies, one may reasonably doubt whether such a task might be accomplished simply by perusing the right book. On the other hand, given the general decline of shared values and even basic civility in contemporary society, *The Spirit of Community* will make a valuable contribution if it achieves nothing more than a spirited debate.

The Detroit News, June 30, 1993

The Sad Irony of the Civil Rights Movement

(*Colored People: A Memoir* by Henry Louis Gates Jr., Alfred Knopf [1994])

While much as been written about the black family in American society and the myriad problems which have appeared in the wake of its slow decline, few books have contained more insight than the recently published *Colored People*. What sets this book apart is that it is not some ponderous, scholarly treatise concerning family values or the role of race in American society, but an intimate, eminently readable chronicle of the early life of its author, Henry Louis Gates Jr., now an English professor and chairman of Afro-American studies at Harvard College.

On one level, *Colored People*, may be read as a memoir about the author and his family. As such, the book is populated by the sorts of colorful, idiosyncratic personalities who inhabit many families (although the Gateses seem to have had more than their fair share). The reader is introduced in breakneck fashion to: the matriarch of the family, his beloved grandmother; his reserved, though surprisingly strong-willed mother; his practical father; and various aunts, uncles, and even neighbors and friends who made up the small West Virginia town of Piedmont where Gates was born in 1950.

On another level, the book has interesting commentary about the carefully ordered world in which so many Americans, black and white, lived during the 1950s. That world was ordered so as to allow individuals whose only real difference was skin pigmentation to co-exist peacefully in the midst of legally-sanctioned segregation. For example, Gates notes that when he was growing up, his family, like other blacks in Piedmont, rented the home in which they lived since it was understood that blacks were not to own property.

In a particularly poignant passage, Gates describes that world from the perspective of black Americans:

> The soul of that world was colored. Its inhabitants went to colored schools, they went to colored churches, they lived in colored neighborhoods, they ate colored food, they listened to colored music, and when all that fat and grease finally closed down their arteries or made their hearts explode, they slept in colored cemeteries, escorted there by colored preachers. They dated colored, married colored, divorced and cheated on colored. And when they could, they taught at colored colleges, preached to colored congregations, trimmed colored hair on nappy heads, and after the fifties, even fought to keep alive the tradition of segregated all-colored schools.

Many events unfolded at a time when American society was on the verge of a painful transition from segregation to something new, but as yet unknown. It was a transition that in retrospect would "evoke a colored world of the fifties, a Negro world of the early sixties, and the advent of a black world of the later sixties." One irony of this transition was that because blacks in Piedmont had become so accustomed to the accommodations made to survive in a segregated world, they viewed the arrival of the civil rights movement and integration with mixed emotions.

"Only later did I come to realize," notes the author, "that for many of the colored people in Piedmont integration was experienced as a loss. The warmth and nurturance of the womblike colored world" slowly, but inevitably, disappeared. The process began in 1956, when the black high school was closed, and culminated when the local mill put a stop to the traditional, company-sponsored black picnic because, in the opinion of company management, "the law forbade separate but equal everything, including picnics."

Another irony was the effect which societal dislocations caused by integration had upon the black family. The author's personal reminiscences remind the reader about the role that the black family once fulfilled so well but, all too often, no longer: extolling to each new generation the virtues of hard work and education as the means by which to achieve success, even in the face of discrimination.

For example, Gates recounts being surrounded by relatives who had gathered to attend his grandfather's funeral:

> That day was a revelation. Doctors and dentists, lawyers and pharmacists; Howard and Talledega, Harvard and Radcliffe—all of these careers and all of these schools were in my grandparents' living room that day, and each had a Gates face attached to it. It came as a shock to realize that these mythic characters in Daddy's tales were actual brown and tan and beige people. And refined. And well spoken. Obviously comfortable in the world.

The generation of the author's parents seemed to accept, almost intuitively, the value of certain propositions that many members of subsequent generations intentionally abandoned as quaint anachronisms: that religious faith is important; that in-tact, two-parent families afforded certain advantages when nurturing children; that citizens should show respect for authority and accept individual responsibility for their actions.

That older generation also seemed to understand that civil society rests upon quite tenuous foundations. As such, they viewed with suspicion the approaching civil rights movement, certainly not because they favored segregation, but because they believed that movement might unleash forces which would undermine values in the existing order that should be preserved. Given the misfortunes which have undertaken much of the black American underclass—the high number of illegitimate births and female-headed households, the prevalence of violent crime and drug abuse, to name but a few—the concerns of that earlier generation appear to have been justified.

Colored People is certainly a thought-provoking book, both as a memoir and as an almost wistful commentary about a black America long gone.

The Detroit News, August 24, 1994

Racism: Civil Rights
and Moral Wrongs

(*The End of Racism* by Dinesh
D'Souza; Free Press [1995])

Few matters of national public policy are more deserving of serious consideration yet more prone to simplistic analysis than that of race in American society.

A generation ago, this country celebrated the passage of the 1964 civil rights act as testament to the principle that all Americans should be judged on the basis of individual merit rather than skin color. Yet many scholars and much of the media now would have us believe that black and white Americans view each other across the chasm of a great racial divide. If the perception is accurate, how did this state of affairs evolve?

A provocative new book entitled *The End of Racism* attempts to provide some answers. The book, written by Dinesh D'Souza, a research fellow at the American Enterprise Institute in Washington, D.C., is by turns analytically eloquent and gratuitously offensive. Over the course of 556 pages, supplemented by another 157 pages of notes, the author develops his theme, the essence of which is that racism in America is essentially a thing of the past. D'Souza defines racism as "an ideology of moral or intellectual superiority based upon the biological characteristics of race. Moreover, racism typically entails a willingness to discriminate based upon a perceived hierarchy of superior and inferior races."

D'Souza begins by tracing the origins of racism, which proves to be a less than efficacious digression. For example, the author consumes an entire chapter attempting to convince the reader that slavery was not a racist institution. Among the evidence proffered by D'Souza in support of this novel proposition is that America was not the first country to engage in the enterprise and that some free blacks also owned slaves. None of this is particularly persuasive for the simple reason that, in the final analysis, slavery was morally wrong—especially in a country founded on the principles of inalienable rights and equal justice under the law—regardless of whether it failed to satisfy some technical definition of racism.

The author stands on firmer ground when examining the origins of the modern civil rights movement and where that movement ultimately went astray. As he perceptively notes, the civil rights movement "arose out of a ferocious debate between W.E.B. Du Bois and Booker T. Washington, two men who represented contrasting strategies of political protest and self-help." In response to the legally-sanctioned segregation which arose in this country in the latter part of the 19th century, Du Bois stressed the importance of securing black civil rights; Washington the importance of cultivating black personal responsibility. The nascent civil rights movement adopted the views of Du Bois over those of Washington, with mixed results.

One result was the impressive string of legal and political victories, such as the *Brown* school desegregation decision, the 1964 Civil Rights Act, and the 1965 Voting Rights Act which achieved the objective of realizing basic rights for black Americans. However, while these early civil rights measures exorcised formal racism from American society, in D'Souza's opinion, they did not produce the equality of results that many had expected, principally because civil rights leaders failed to simultaneously stress personal responsibility within the black community:

> Once the activists who fought alongside Martin Luther King, Jr. secured the color-blind regime they demanded, they probably should have focused on the strict enforcement of nondiscrim-

ination combined with a civic mission to raise the
civilization standards of the black community.
They rejected this path, however, and denounced
those who raised the issue of black cultural defects
as racists and enemies of black progress.

In turn, the failure of civil rights leaders to stress personal
responsibility spawned many of the misfortunes that have overtaken
much of the black underclass—the high number of illegitimate births
and female-headed households, the prevalence of violent crime and
drug abuse, to name but a few. As the author notes, these "conspic-
uous pathologies of blacks are the products of catastrophic cultural
changes that pose a threat both to the African-American community
and to society at large. These pathologies are far more serious than
the fact that, for whatever reason, there are too few black math pro-
fessors and nuclear physicists."

D'Souza argues that most African-American scholars simply
refuse to acknowledge the pathology of violence in the black underclass, apparently convinced that black criminals, as well as their targets,
are both victims. To the contrary, such scholars argue that the real cul-
prit is societal racism and that the answer lies in federal jobs programs
and recruitment into the private sector. "Yet it seems unrealistic, bor-
dering on the surreal, to imagine underclass blacks with their gold
chains, limping walk, obscene language, and arsenal of weapons doing
nine-to-five jobs at Proctor and Gamble or the State Department."
Despite the somewhat intemperate phraseology, D'Souza has a point.

Indeed, the author contends that instead of honestly acknowl-
edging the problems confronting the black community, civil rights
leaders simply abandoned their historic commitment to equal rights
in favor of a new objective: equality of condition measured by proportional representation of minorities in such areas as hiring, pro-
motions, and college admissions. In bringing about this dramatic
change in focus from color-blindness to color-conscious, civil rights
activists were aided by sympathetic federal courts and executive

agency bureaucrats who intentionally went about their task shielded from public scrutiny:

> The reason for this reluctance to provide full disclosure is clear. Martin Luther King, Jr., had just led a civil rights revolution based on the moral necessity of erasing race from the entire fabric of American laws and policies. Liberal policymakers and civil rights activists recognized how difficult it would be to attempt to undo the public consensus on color-blindness.

Needless to say, such sentiments are not likely to endear D'Souza to the leadership of the contemporary civil rights establishment. No doubt the feeling will be mutual.

The author makes little effort to veil his opinions concerning the shortcomings of that leadership:

> Many black activist who once came from poor and rural backgrounds have found, upon winning their battles for legal equality, that they do not wish to return to obscurity. In the civil rights establishment, these activists have found a way to turn racial victimization, which was their historical condition, into a successful career. Having come to do good, they have stayed to do well.

Given the blunt manner in which *The End of Racism* makes its case, many civil rights leaders may conclude in retrospect that Murray and Hernstein's *The Bell Curve* was not that bad a book after all.

The Detroit News, October 18, 1995

Part 2

Voices Columns

Election Affirmed Founders' Wisdom

The inauguration of George W. Bush as the 43rd president of the United States was preceded by what was, in many respects, an eminently forgettable presidential campaign. However, the campaign and the inauguration served as bookends to a remarkable post-election interlude which revealed much, not just about the character of the man who had aspired to lead the national government, but also about how little many citizens understand about the nature of that government.

That interlude revealed in Albert Gore a singular ambition which propelled an unseemly refusal to accept defeat, an unseemliness not exhibited since the election of 1800. In that year, a historical fluke resulted in Thomas Jefferson and his vice-presidential running mate, Aaron Burr, each receiving 73 electoral votes. When Burr refused to concede the presidency, the election was decided in favor of Jefferson by the House of Representatives, but not until that body had voted thirty-six times and the nation had endured considerable uncertainty. A similar result might have obtained 200 years later had the U.S. Supreme Court not offered salutary intervention. That Gore, or Burr for that matter, may have been within his rights in contesting a close election misses the mark. Legalisms aside, as the British understand, some things (asking a lady her age, buttoning the bottom button of one's suit vest, and until recently in our country, contesting a presidential election) simply aren't done because they suggest a disregard for societal customs and traditions.

Of greater importance, post-election events revealed the lack of familiarity which many Americans have with the nature of the government under which we live. Witness the confusion regarding the purpose, or even the existence, of the Electoral College, or the surprise expressed by many upon learning that presidents are not selected by popular vote.

The Founding Fathers feared the concentration of too much governmental power in any one set of hands, even that of the people themselves. In his masterful analysis of human nature in Federalist No. 10, James Madison described the tendency of societies to degenerate into special interests and, where those interests were shared by a majority of citizens, of the temptation for the majority to trample upon the rights of the minority. This tendency was magnified in democracies because the people held the reins of government directly. "Hence it is," Madison noted, "that such democracies have ever been spectacles of turbulence and contention; have ever been found incompatible with personal security or the rights of property; and have in general been as short in their lives as they have been violent in their deaths."

The remedy for this inherent tendency toward faction was to establish, not a democracy, but a republic, the latter being distinguished from the former by the concept of representation. The Founders believed that a government in which the will of the people was expressed through an intermediary of elected representatives rather than by the people themselves would afford greater protection for individual liberties by being less susceptible to the passions of the moment, or to the intrigues of enterprising individuals who masked personal ambition as public service. Properly understood, constitutional devices such as the Electoral College, rather than being arcane relics, are an integral part of our system of government. Other such devices include the diffusion of governmental power between the states and a limited central government, and the further diffusion of the latter power among coordinate, but separate, branches which serve as checks and balances upon each other.

Changes to our national Constitution over its 213-year history have introduced democratic elements into our republican form of government. Some of those changes undeniably have been beneficial (e.g., the Thirteenth, Fourteenth, and Fifteenth Amendments, which ended slavery, guaranteed an equal protection of the laws to all citizens, and ensured unabridged voting rights, respectively), while others have proven less so (e.g., the Sixteenth Amendment, which institutionalized class envy through federal income taxation). However, ours remains, at its heart, a republic, which depends not only upon the consent of the governed, but also upon an abiding responsibility of the governed to understand the nature of their government.

Lansing State Journal, January 25, 2001

Overburdened Taxpayers
Deserve Relief

Candidate George W. Bush promised to reduce the federal tax burden on American citizens by $1.6 trillion over the next decade, a promise which, happily, President George W. Bush seems determined to keep. The main thrust of the Bush tax plan consists of reducing marginal tax rates, reducing the number of tax brackets from five to four, eliminating the so-called marriage penalty whereby working spouses filing jointly pay more in federal income taxes than both combined would pay as single individuals, and phasing out the federal estate tax.

Earlier this month, the House of Representatives passed the rate reduction portion of the plan—albeit in a watered down form—and sent it on to the Senate. It remains to be seen whether the "world's greatest deliberative body" will follow suit or will, as is often its wont, show much deliberation but little greatness.

That a reduction in federal taxes is in order would seem beyond reasonable disagreement. After all, federal taxes as a percentage of gross domestic product are higher today (20.5 percent) than at any other time in our nation's history except during war. Nevertheless, the President's remarkably modest proposal—it would amount to less than a third of the estimated $5.6 trillion in federal surpluses expected over the next decade—has engendered the predictable reaction from the Washington ruling class, which never seems so discomfited as by the thought that average citizens should presume to retain what they earn.

Liberals, and some moderate Republicans, contend that the federal government cannot "afford" to cut taxes, at least not now, or at least not in the amount proposed by the President. Rather, they argue that the national debt first should be retired, unmet needs should be addressed and, of course, tax relief should be targeted to those most in need. That such arguments are made despite the President having also proposed to earmark $2 trillion for debt retirement and another $1 trillion for contingencies, and to remove six million additional individuals from the federal tax rolls, suggests that they are not to be taken seriously.

Regrettably, the President has not assisted his own case by characterizing tax relief as a tonic to stimulate the softening national economy, a line of reasoning which essentially would relegate tax relief to times of recession. A more salient reason to commend a reduction in federal taxes is that governmental surpluses should be returned collectively to the taxpayers who produced them, a point which Mr. Bush has, upon occasion, expressed with elegant simplicity.

That the government might wish to utilize surplus revenues to achieve its own ends should be of no consequence. Consider what your reaction might be, after having been grossly overcharged by your auto mechanic, for example, to be informed that the excess, rather than being returned to you would be used instead to assist more deserving customers. Yet, what is the federal surplus if not the sum total of overcharges upon the American people, based upon a sliding scale according to income?

Furthermore, the sphere of individual liberty is enhanced in proportion to which the sphere of government is limited. One of the most effective means of limiting government is by limiting that which constitutes its lifeblood, namely taxes. Hence, the perennial struggle between government, the nature of which is to grow ever larger and more intrusive, and the governed, whose interests lie in restricting their government within acceptable boundaries; history suggests it to be a struggle in which the governed rarely prevail.

Each year, the Washington-based Tax Foundation calculates "tax freedom day." During 2000, that date did not occur until the 124th day of the year, meaning that the nation's taxpayers had to work from January 1st through May 3rd just to pay all federal, state, and local taxes. Stated another way, on average, Americans spend more time working to pay taxes than to provide food, clothing, and shelter combined. Consider that the next time the Washington ruling class waxes poetic concerning how it cannot afford to reduce taxes.

Lansing State Journal, March 22, 2001

"Leaders" Let Down Black Americans

Contrary to conventional wisdom, African Americans tend to be rather conservative on a range of issues. To cite but two examples, opinion surveys consistently reveal their substantial support for tough crime measures and school choice, no doubt reflecting the fact that many African Americans reside in communities in which high crime rates and academically deficient schools predominate.

Given these views, it might have been thought that George W. Bush would have done quite well among African American voters in the last presidential election. Not only was there his track record as governor of Texas of successfully reaching out to minority voters, but also his presidential campaign mantra of compassionate conservatism. In fact, however, African American voters again proved to be one of the most reliable mainstays of the political left. Mr. Bush received but eight percent of the African-American vote, a smaller percentage than that received by any other GOP presidential candidate since Barry Goldwater garnered six percent in 1964.

That so many African Americans so often vote contrary to their own interests stands as a testament to the continued sway wielded by the civil rights establishment. In 1955, English author Henry Fairlie coined the proper noun "the Establishment" to describe the group of prominent individuals, such as the Archbishop of Canterbury, whom Fairlie considered to be the actual rulers of Great Britain. It is characteristic of an establishment that it claims to speak for others while, in fact, skillfully, even ingeniously, pursuing its own interests.

So it is with the civil rights establishment. The transparent self-promotion exhibited by the leaders of that establishment (one thinks of Jesse Jackson, Al Sharpton, and California Congresswoman Maxine Waters, for example) would be objectionable enough even were it not accompanied by their routine presumption to speak for all African Americans on matters of race. That those leaders tend to be as reliably liberal in their views as many rank and file African Americans tend to be conservative in theirs is often obscured by cleverly orchestrated appeals to racial solidarity.

Indeed, many in the civil rights establishment have built their careers by portraying minorities in general, and African Americans in particular, as hapless victims of a racist society, victims who can succeed only with the assistance of massive governmental programs and preferential treatment. In doing so, they have found a congenial home within the party of the New Deal and the Great Society, but at the price of having reduced the once proud civil rights movement to little more than a wholly owned subsidiary of the modern welfare state.

Furthermore, the civil rights establishment has squandered much of the precious moral capital which propelled the civil rights movement by pursuing matters whose symbolism is exceeded only by their utter inconsequentiality. Consider the resources that have been expended opposing confederate flag displays, for example (as if the destiny of 36 million Americans is somehow to be thwarted by a piece of cloth) or promoting slavery reparations which, ironically, amount to little more than racial profiling.

At the same time, the civil rights establishment has failed to address with any discernible enthusiasm problems pandemic to much of the African American community such as drug addiction, high crime rates, illegitimacy, and poor educational achievement. And, too often, proposals which might effectively address some of these problems, proposals such as welfare reform, vouchers, or emphasizing personal responsibility, generally have been dismissed by the civil rights establishment as "conservative" ideas.

The previous generation of civil rights leaders, men such as Dr. Martin Luther King, Jr., Roy Wilkins, and Whitney Young, did not mortgage the fortunes of the civil rights movement to one political party or political philosophy. They were willing to consider any point of view that might advance the noble cause in which they were engaged. Nor, did they toil for preferential treatment, but for equal treatment for all before the law; not to promote themselves, but to improve the lot of all Americans. Until the current civil rights establishment embraces that same spirit, it will continue to do a disservice to those it purports to serve.

Lansing State Journal, May 17, 2001

Courts Should Read Law, Not Write Policy

In Federalist No. 78, Alexander Hamilton observed that of the three branches of government, the judiciary was the least dangerous to the rights of the people because it had influence over neither the sword (as did the executive) nor the purse (as did the legislative). It generally was accepted in Hamilton's day that courts were to fulfill the limited role of declaring what the law was, within the context of particular legal disputes and based upon an established set of legal principles. In short, the courts were to vindicate private rights, such those of contract or of property, while leaving to the popularly elected branches, or to the people, the advancement of public policy through in the enactment of laws.

Times have changed. Commencing with the New Deal, the sphere of judicial influence has greatly expanded, rendering obsolete Montesquieu's observation that the judicial power is "next to nothing." Indeed, over the last half century, liberals increasingly have taken the position that judges should not limit themselves to traditional notions of judicial authority, but should be free to wield powers reserved under our form of government to the policymaking branches, the implication being that courts, federal courts in particular, should act as agents of social change.

One consequence of this view has been an increased divisiveness surrounding the selection of judges. Witness how contentious has become the confirmation process for federal judicial nominees, or the vitriol which characterized much of last year's campaign for the Michigan Supreme Court. The corrosive effect upon the judiciary has been as inevitable as it has been regrettable. However, if judges are to be no more than policymakers clad in black robes, free to impose upon society their personal predilections in the guise of legal pronouncements, then the judiciary scarcely can claim exemption from the rough and tumble which attends partisan politics.

In light of decades of judicial activism, it is appropriate to restate certain principles which are fundamental to American constitutional thinking and practice. First, it is conducive to individual liberty that governmental power be dispersed among distinct branches so as to prevent its concentration in any one institution. Within this framework, the role of the judiciary is, and should be, limited to construing the law. History suggests that intervention by the courts in matters best left to the political branches (such as the 1857 *Dred Scott* decision which accorded constitutional protection to slavery or the 1973 *Roe* decision which decreed a constitutional right to abortion) has largely proven disastrous, both for the country and the courts.

Second, in construing the law, courts should accord it the meaning intended by those by whom the law was framed. When the law is clear and unambiguous on its face, no interpretation is necessary. However, where a provision of law permits of more than one interpretation, the courts should deduce its meaning through a principled reading of the text itself.

For example, it would be difficult to conceive of a court resolving a simple breach of contract dispute without attempting to determine the intent of the parties as conveyed by the words of the contract itself. Yet, what is the law, particularly a constitution, if not the most fundamental of contracts, between not mere private parties but the people and their government?

That judicial activists find fault in so commonsense an approach is no small measure of the affliction which disorders their thinking. For, in the final analysis judicial activism not only infringes upon the policymaking branches; it also deprives citizens of the benefits of what the judiciary was intended to be: an objective arbiter of legal disputes.

Lansing State Journal, July 12, 2001

Restore Fairness to Heart
of Civil Rights Fight

Two generations ago, our nation celebrated passage of the 1964 Civil Rights Act, a landmark piece of legislation intended to ensure that minorities would be accorded equality before the law. Although not uncontroversial, the legislation was supported by a broad coalition including veterans' groups, religious leaders, organized labor, and in Congress, Republicans and northern Democrats. Southern Democrats, for the most part, opposed passage. The legislation was a testament to a principle which all too often had been honored in the breach: that all Americans should be judged on the basis of merit rather than skin color.

In the years intervening since 1964, however, the continuing debate over race and civil rights has become increasingly rancorous, the tone at times anything but civil. Rather than agreement, often there appears to be greater division. Indeed, the very term "affirmative action" which, when first used in a 1961 presidential executive order, meant that employers should take affirmative steps to recruit minorities who might not otherwise apply because of past discrimination, has since become synonymous with reverse discrimination and quotas. And a recent national poll found that 52 percent of white Americans surveyed believed that too much attention is paid to racial issues, while 64 percent of African Americans felt that such issues receive too little attention. What, then, has happened to the national consensus out of which the 1964 Civil Rights Act was forged, and why?

One answer is to be found in the expectation of some civil rights activists that the guarantee of equality before the law would lead to equality of opportunity which, in turn, would lead to equality of condition. That this expectation never was realistic, given the differing motivations, ambitions, talents, and abilities of individuals, did not prevent the expectation from being held. Nor did lessons from history illustrating that when equality of condition had been attempted, as under socialism, the result usually had been an equality of destitution. Thus, when the expectation was not realized, civil rights activists turned to equality of condition as the goal outright.

A major turning point came in 1971, with the U.S. Supreme Court decision in *Griggs* vs. *Duke Power Company*. At issue was the company's requirement that all job applicants take a standardized test and possess at least a high school diploma. The court held that such neutral employment criteria were presumptively illegal if they produced a "disparate impact" adverse to minorities. Because, for whatever reason, African Americans as a group did not perform as well as did white Americans on standardized tests and were less likely to have a high school diploma, the employer bore the burden of proving that these criteria were job related. The fact that an employer might prefer high school graduates because it found them generally to be more productive, and more highly motivated as employees, was of no consequence.

The *Griggs* decision placed the imprimatur of federal courts upon the notion that statistical evidence of disparate impact was as important, if not more so, than proof of actual discrimination based upon racial bias in hiring. It also shifted the emphasis from alleged acts of discrimination against individuals to whether individuals were members of a particular racial or ethnic group. Disparate impact against racial and ethnic groups ushered in numerical goals and quotas, which, eventually, ushered in notions of enforced diversity.

Public support for affirmative action waned as the public began to realize that what once was about equality under law had become little more than a racial spoils system. The manner by which to regain that support is to again make basic fairness the goal of affirmative action.

Lansing State Journal, September 6, 2001

America Must Defend
Western Traditions

Several weeks after the terrorist attacks of September 11ᵗʰ, Italian Prime Minister Silvio Berlusconi caused quite a stir throughout much of the international community by expressing the view that Western civilization is superior to that of Islamic nations. The Secretary General of the Arab League quickly demanded an apology, accusing the Prime Minister of having "crossed the limits of reason and decency." Several of Mr. Berlusconi's colleagues in the European Union, which has elevated political correctness to an international art form, reacted in similar fashion. For example, Belgian Foreign Minister Louis Michel condemned the remarks, while the Belgian Prime Minister expressed incredulity that someone could make such a statement.

However, aside from having offended the tender sensibilities of moral relativists, to whom it is heresy even to suggest that all cultures are not of equal worth, it is not readily apparent why Berlusconi's remarks should have engendered such a harsh reaction. After all, the Prime Minister was not denigrating Islamic civilization so much as expressing a preference for Western traditions of classical liberalism. What Berlusconi said was that:

> We have to be conscious of the strength of our civilization; we cannot put the two civilizations on the same level. All of the achievements of our civilization: free institutions, the love of liberty itself—which represents our greatest asset—the liberty of the individual and the liberty of peo-

ples. These, certainly, are not the inheritance of other civilizations such as Islamic civilization.

While perhaps indelicately put, the Italian Prime Minister's comments accurately reflect the political reality throughout the Middle East. One can search from Saudi Arabia, to Egypt, to Jordan, to Syria, for example, without finding democratic governmental traditions, at least of contemporary vintage. Indeed, among the countries of that region, only Israel has a government which is popularly elected.

More importantly, Berlusconi's comments served as a timely reminder of why the war on terrorism, upon which our nation has embarked, is worth waging. That which hangs in the balance is not merely bringing to justice those who committed craven acts against American citizens, and others, but preserving a way of life that indisputably is worth preserving. Limited, representative government, and its corollary, individual liberty, are quintessential elements of Western political tradition. The uniquely American contribution to this tradition consists of having understood that the most effective means by which to secure individual liberties was to reduce the basic framework of government to a written document, the Constitution, which would serve as the supreme law of the land.

Americans have lived under a written constitution for so long as to take for granted the blessings it has made possible: freedom of speech and of the press, freedom to practice one's religion and to criticize one's government, equality before the law, the notion that a just government rests upon the consent of the governed, and unparalleled economic prosperity which could not have been achieved in the absence of political liberty. Yet, only belatedly, if at all, have other countries come to appreciate, and to emulate, the simple innovation of a written constitution. Nearly two thirds of the world's constitutions have been adopted since 1970. In fact, fewer than 20 of them were adopted before World War II, and no other nation's constitution predates that of the United States.

America long has stood as the exemplar of the Western traditions of free political and economic institutions of which the Italian

Prime Minister spoke. The people of the Middle East deserve the opportunity to partake of all the benefits which those traditions have to bestow once, that is, the war on terrorism is won.

Lansing State Journal, November 1, 2001

For America, Life Isn't Completely New

This column is noteworthy for several reasons having (candor compels the admission) nothing to do with its content. This is the final Voices column of 2001 and, indeed, the final Voices column period, this newspaper having announced last month its decision to discontinue such columns in lieu of a different arrangement. It would be an inexcusable breach of manners not to express appreciation for the honor of having had the opportunity, throughout this year, to offer commentary upon public affairs, particularly given the momentous events to which our nation has been witness during the last twelve months.

This year began with the inauguration of a new president whose very claim to office was questioned by many; it ends with the nation having embarked upon a war unlike any other in its history—one which must be won if that history is to continue—a war made unavoidable by the events of September 11th.

It has been said that the events of that day changed everything. Well, yes and no. Two examples, one concerning foreign policy, the other, domestic politics, will suffice.

The foreign policy of the Bush administration has, to date, been characterized by a clarity not seen in Washington since the presidency of Ronald Reagan. Like Reagan, George W. Bush seems guided by common sense, good judgment, and a refreshing lack of concern about the opinions of political elites either in this country or in the capitals of Europe. Thus, the President announced early on his intention not to participate in the flawed Kyoto global warming treaty and recently made good on his pledge to withdraw from the 1972 Anti-Ballistic Missile Treaty, a document so outdated that the only other signatory to it (the Soviet Union) no longer even exists.

But, perhaps nowhere has the Bush clarity been more evident than in dealing with the Middle East conflict. A succession of diplomats, including American secretaries of state, have beaten a path to that region, calling for an end to the "cycle of violence" as if there were some moral equivalence between Palestinian terrorist acts against innocent Israeli civilians, on the one hand, and defensive responses by the Israeli government against the perpetrators of those acts, on the other. The violent attacks upon our own soil, and our response to them, have rendered untenable any contention that Israel should not have the same right to defend itself against terrorism that America has exercised since September 11th. The President seemed to have concluded as much as evidenced by his loss of patience with Yasser Arafat.

Meanwhile, at home, the chairperson of the U.S. Civil Rights Commission seems determined to prove, once again, that she is neither civil nor a respecter of the rights of others with whom she disagrees. Mary Frances Berry has refused to seat on the commission Peter Kirsanow, appointed by President Bush to succeed Victoria Wilson, a Clinton appointee whose term expired on November 29th. As justification for her refusal to recognize Mr. Kirsanow's appointment, Berry has concocted the preposterous argument that Wilson was appointed to a full six-year term rather than to serve out the remainder of the term of Leon Higginbotham, who died in 1998.

However, it would appear that the real objection of Ms. Berry to Mr. Kirsanow who, like herself, is African American, is that he is not the right sort of African American; he is conservative and a Republican. The latter consideration is not insignificant as the commission presently is comprised of four Democrats and three Republicans. The addition of Mr. Kirsanow will prevent Ms. Berry from continuing to use the commission as a personal platform from which to pursue political correctness.

Perhaps Ms. Berry senses that the Bush administration, in concert with, as Lincoln put it, "the silent artillery of time," has rendered her as irrelevant to civil rights as is Yasser Arafat to peace in the Middle East.

Lansing State Journal, December 27, 2001

Part 3

Miscellaneous Commentaries

Liberals' Case Against
Bork Falls Short

The rhetoric of the far left would have us believe that the appointment of Robert Bork to the U.S. Supreme Court virtually would mean the end of Western civilization as we know it. As a conservative who happens to be black, I thought it was time someone examined the facts and set the record straight. Although liberals and special interest groups advance several reasons for opposing Bork, none of these stand up under scrutiny.

There is no doubt that Bork has impeccable intellectual and judicial credentials. He has been a law professor, a former U.S. solicitor general and since 1982, a judge on the U.S. Appeals Court for the District of Columbia. The U.S. Supreme Court has overturned not one of the more than 100 majority decisions written by Bork—nor any of the more than the 300 decisions in which he has concurred.

Nevertheless, critics say he is too conservative. The irony is that Bork believes a judge's personal views should not influence how cases are decided. Indeed, he believes judges—especially federal judges, who are unelected—should decide cases solely on the basis of legal principles found in the Constitution.

Another argument that critics such as Joseph Biden, chairman of the Senate Judiciary Committee, make is that the law should not be a pendulum that swings back and forth. The implication is that Bork would overrule important affirmative action and abortion rights cases.

No one would deny that courts should respect long-established and case-hardened precedents. But what liberals are really saying is that recent precedents with which they agree should never be overruled.

If liberals are consistent in their views, then they must regret that in 1954 the Warren Court struck down the separate-but-equal doctrine of *Plessey* vs *Ferguson*. That doctrine had stood for 58 years—longer than any precedent established by the Warren court and certainly longer than the 14-year old *Roe* vs *Wade* abortion decision. But the Warren Court properly struck down *Plessey* vs *Ferguson* because it was not in keeping with our most important constitutional principle: equality before the law.

It is also said that the current ideological balance of the court must be maintained, meaning moderate former Justice Lewis Powell must be replaced with another moderate. One will search both the Constitution and American history in vain to find support for this new-fangled notion.

If the court's ideological balance could never be altered, we would now have a court that would be ideologically identical to the first Supreme Court. The irony is that it is doubtful that the six original justices supported affirmative action, women's rights or any other issue liberals hold dear.

Indeed, adhering to this theory would mean Franklin Roosevelt had no authority to appoint liberals such as William Douglas or Felix Frankfurter to replace the conservative "nine old men," who had invalidated so much of the New Deal legislation in the 1930s. Likewise, the liberal Earl Warren, who helped usher in many of the decisions liberals cherish, should not have been appointed in 1953 to replace the more conservative Chief Justice Fred Vinson.

Sen. Biden seeks to use this new "constitutional" theory to explain his recent change of heart. He had said some months ago that if Reagan were to nominate someone as qualified as Bork, he would vote for the nominee. Of course, Biden has since recanted, since he is running for the Democratic presidential nomination and liberal special interest groups are making opposition to Bork a litmus test for support. When the president did nominate someone as qualified as Bork—Bork himself—Biden explained that what he had meant was that he would vote for Bork to replace another conservative justice. Okay, then why did he and other Senate Democrats attack Justice

William Rehnquist when he was nominated to succeed conservative Chief Justice Warren Burger?

Liberals also are attempting to get mileage from a 1963 Bork article questioning the propriety of some provisions of what would become the Civil Rights Act of 1964. Bork long ago publicly admitted that he was incorrect and that the law was good for the country. Whatever Bork's alleged deficiencies, he has shown himself capable of admitting mistakes.

Besides, few justices have held views that were completely beyond reproach. The late Hugo Black, who staunchly supported school desegregation on the court, had formerly been a member of the Ku Klux Klan in Alabama. Warren championed civil liberties and the rights of the accused, even though he strenuously supported Franklin Roosevelt's detention of Japanese-Americans in relocation camps as California attorney general during World War II—even though there was no evidence of disloyalty. As Warren biographer Jack Harrison Pollock put it, "Perhaps the kindest thing that can be said for Warren and the entire nation is that both later had the grace to be ashamed."

While the Senate has the power to be capricious on confirmations, its role traditionally has been to pass on the intellectual, judicial and moral qualifications of a nominee. As if to underscore this role, rarely has the Senate rejected a Supreme Court nominee purely on ideological grounds. Only twice in this century—in 1930 with Hoover nominee John Parker and in 1970 with Nixon nominee G. Harrold Carswell—has the senate rejected a president's authority to nominate individuals who share his views. And the votes were close: 41-39 against Parker and 51-45 against Carswell.

A president has an obligation to select the person who is in his judgment most qualified to serve on the court, an obligation President Reagan has fulfilled by nominating Judge Bork. The American people elected Reagan in 1980 and overwhelmingly re-elected him in 1984, knowing his views on the role of the federal judiciary. In fact, it was Walter Mondale who made sure court appointments became an important issue in the race.

The fact that Democrats gained control of the Senate in 1986 is of no significance since mid-term elections are often decided on local rather than national issues. If Democrats wish to nominate an otherwise qualified individual whose ideology they prefer, the constitution provides a means. They can get their candidate elected president.

The Detroit News, September 20, 1987

Thomas' Opponents Show
Their True Colors

The nomination of Clarence Thomas to the U.S. Supreme Court comes at a most interesting time. The country is in the midst of an often heated debate over affirmative action and civil rights. If confirmed by the Senate, the conservative Thomas would succeed the liberal Thurgood Marshall, a revered figure in the civil rights movement who recently announced his retirement from the court. In many ways, these two black Americans, both of whom have personally experienced discrimination, epitomize very different views of how that debate should be resolved.

The reaction to the nomination from liberals and many special interest groups has been sadly predictable. The National Organization for Women denounced the nomination as "an insult to Thurgood Marshall and the civil rights community." Senate Majority Leader George Mitchell accused the president of opposing quotas except for Supreme Court nominations, referring to Bush's veto last year of a bill which the president believed would have resulted in hiring quotas. The implication that Thomas was nominated solely because he is black is not only hypocritical coming from liberals, who virtually demanded that Bush nominate another minority to success Marshall, but also unfair to Thomas.

Before he was appointed to the U.S. Court of Appeals for the District of Columbia in early 1990, Thomas served for nearly a decade in the Reagan and Bush administrations, as an assistant attorney general and later as chairman of the Equal Employment Opportunity Commission. Although Thomas has only been a federal judge for about 16 months, many individuals have lacked extensive judicial experience when they were nominated to the Supreme Court. William Brennan had not served as a federal judge when he was nominated to the court. Nor had Earl Warren ever served in any judicial capacity when he was appointed chief justice. Surely liberals are not suggesting that the conservative grandson of a Georgia share-cropper should satisfy a higher standard than a white nominee with liberal views?

Critics also contend that Thomas should be rejected because another conservative appointee will further shift the ideological balance of the court. To the extent this concern is valid, it cannot be addressed by rejecting Thomas because the president would likely nominate someone else just as conservative. The changing ideological balance on the court is the inevitable result of Democrats having lost five of the last six presidential elections. To make matters worse, Jimmy Carter, the only Democrat who did win during this period, was also the first president to leave office without making an appointment to the court since Andrew Johnson left the White House in 1869.

The concern that liberals have expressed about a conservative court is that it will overturn existing precedent. In particular, abortion rights groups fear the imminent demise of *Roe* vs. *Wade*. Thomas has indeed criticized the tortured holding of *Roe*—as distinguished from its result—but so have legal scholars on various sides of the abortion issue. In any event, criticizing the reasoning in the case does not necessarily reflect a desire to overturn the result.

The irony of the liberal argument about precedent is that many of the landmark decisions that have changed our society for the better, such as the 1954 *Brown* school desegregation decision, were possible only because the court was willing to examine the precedent. After all, the court is not infallible. Those who would worship at the altar of precedent should take the long view and recall that it was the court which once declared blacks had "no rights that the white man was bound to respect" and which legally enshrined the separate but equal doctrine in American society for 58 years.

Most interesting, perhaps, has been the reaction that the Thomas nomination has drawn from the civil rights establishment.

The leaders of that establishment, who all too frequently presume to speak for all black Americans, seem genuinely baffled by the thought that a black person could be philosophically conservative.

For example, Noah Griffin, an editor of the San Francisco Examiner, has referred to Thomas as a "quisling who appears to have forgotten where he came from." This reaction is neither isolated, nor altogether surprising given the disproportionate amount of capital that the civil rights establishment and other liberals have invested in portraying blacks as victims of society who can only succeed with the help of massive government programs and preferential treatment.

Thomas is viewed as a threat by many liberals because he has dared to challenge this orthodoxy. He has been an outspoken critic of preferential treatment and racial quotas, arguing that the Constitution must be interpreted in a colorblind fashion.

That the present civil rights establishment finds fault with such views suggests how far it has strayed from the original goals of the civil rights movement. That movement was not about preferential treatment, but about equality for all before the law. Clarence Thomas and other black conservatives, among whose number I count myself, are not only products of that proud movement, but the true heirs of its philosophy.

Thurgood Marshall has been a tireless champion of civil rights throughout his life. His efforts have made this a better country for everyone, particularly for black Americans. It is no show of disrespect for Marshall's achievements that Americans—even black Americans—might hold diverse views about how best to, in Lincoln's words, "finish up the work we are in." The only tragedy will be if the current civil rights establishment, which prides itself in promoting diversity, has no room at the inn for the opinions of black conservatives.

The Detroit News, August 4, 1991

Media Overstate Problem in Iraq Downplay Progress

During the Civil War, Lincoln is said to have remarked that he had two great enemies, the confederate army in front and financial institutions in the rear, and that of the two, the latter was his greatest foe. One wonders whether President Bush harbors similar sentiments concerning the Iraq war given that, at times, he too seems beset by two opponents: Iraqi insurgents in front and much of the national media in the rear.

Whether from antipathy to the war, or to the administration prosecuting it, the media has found it increasingly difficult to maintain that it has been an impartial chronicler of events. Pretensions to that role have been belied by disproportionate media coverage of situations that place the war in a dubious light and the virtual media shunning of American military successes on the battlefield or in rebuilding Iraqi schools, hospitals, and institutions. And in the media's preoccupation with the number of American military casualties, one senses in the almost daily tabulation an actual purpose of exploiting the casualties to question the efficacy of the war.

For example, this newspaper recently ran the front page headline "U.S. deaths in Iraq pass 1,000" above an Associated Press story. Characteristically, the story did not mourn those lost, nor offer solicitude for their families, but instead emphasized—twice in a mere 233-words—that the majority of the casualties had occurred since President Bush declared an end to major combat operations. One wonders what today's media would have made of the horrendous losses during the Civil War, and of the implication for Lincoln, and the nation, of media coverage prone to magnify every military setback as a wartime president sought desperately to preserve the Union and end slavery.

In 1864, after a succession of inept generals who either could not, or would not, fight, Lincoln gave command of Union forces to Ulysses Grant who proceeded to lose during a single six-week period 52,000 men (nearly equaling the 58,178 American casualties to be suffered during the Vietnam War). At the battle of Cold Harbor, Grant lost 9,000 men in *one hour*; 7,000 of them, as *U.S. News and World Report* writer Michael Barone recently noted in a *Wall Street Journal* article, in the first twenty minutes of fighting. However, in the face of enormous pressure (even from the First Lady) calling for Grant's removal, Lincoln replied in Grant's defense, "I cannot spare him. He fights!"

In his second inaugural, Lincoln remarked upon the origins of the Civil War by observing that one side "would make war rather than let the nation survive; and the other would accept war rather than let it perish. And the war came." On a bright, sunny morning, 136 years, six months, and seven days later, another war came and another administration accepted it rather than let this nation perish or permit the Iraqi people to continue to suffer a brutal tyranny. This war, the war on terror, of which the Iraq war is part and parcel, must be fought if the principles for which America stands are to survive.

Lansing State Journal, September 15, 2004

Obamacare Will Stretch the Government's Tentacles Too Far

On September 17, 1787, as Benjamin Franklin emerged from the Pennsylvania Statehouse after the federal Constitution had been signed, someone asked him, "What type of government have you given us?" He replied that we had been given a republic if, he cautioned, we could keep it. The United States Supreme Court's recent Obamacare decision affords us an opportune moment to hit the pause button and assess whether we have, indeed, "kept" the government we were given. For properly understood, both Obamacare and the decision upholding it are less about health care than about the nature and scope of our government.

In *NFIB* vs *Sebelius*, three conservative justices (Scalia, Thomas, and Alito), and moderate justice Anthony Kennedy, joined Chief Justice Roberts in concluding that Congress exceeded its authority under the federal commerce clause in attempting to require otherwise uninsured Americans to purchase health insurance. However, four liberal justices (Ginsburg, Breyer, Kagan, and Sotomayor) joined Roberts in upholding this individual mandate as a valid exercise of congressional taxing authority.

Given the disparate coalitions of justices who supported different portions of the Chief Justice's opinion, the majority of media attention and commentary has focused on the central role played by Roberts. How, it has been asked, could he in any principled manner find the individual mandate to be unauthorized under one provision of the federal Constitution (i.e., the commerce clause) only to then uphold it under another provision (i.e., the taxing power) and this after having concluded for statutory interpretation purposes that the mandate was not a tax?

However, that the four most liberal justices would have upheld the individual mandate as constitutional on all grounds has been paid scant attention. Justice Ginsburg best expressed her personal view concerning the power of Congress when she noted that "[w]hatever one thinks of the policy decision Congress made [in adopting Obamacare], it was Congress' prerogative to make it." She seemed untroubled by the fact that this was the first time Congress had claimed authority to force citizens to purchase a product against their will, and equally unburdened by any appreciation for the basic proposition that Congress has only that authority granted to it by the federal Constitution.

Indeed, throughout the first 23 pages of her dissent, Ginsburg made no more than passing reference to the very document she was being called upon to construe: the federal Constitution. She chose instead to focus upon health care in general and to laud Obamacare as but the most recent effort by Congress to enact, in her view, socially beneficial legislation. Hers was a focus better suited to a member of the legislative branch than to a member of the judiciary, which is why the four conservative justices dismissed her "exposition of the wonderful things" the federal government had accomplished in the past as being "quite beside the point." However, Justice Ginsburg's view that the federal Constitution affords no effective limitation upon what the federal government may do is entirely of a piece with the philosophy of progressivism.

This November will mark the centennial anniversary of Woodrow Wilson's election as the nation's 28th president. A staunch proponent of progressivism, Wilson openly criticized the Madisonian system of checks and balances established by the Founders to protect individual liberties by limiting government. Wilson's complaint was not that these constitutional features were ineffective, but that they posed an obstacle to progressives whose desire was not to keep the republic, but to replace it with an ever-expanding welfare state. Wilson's New Freedom was the philosophical foundation upon which FDR erected his New Deal and, in turn, LBJ his Great Society. Obamacare is but the latest progressive monstrosity built upon what remains of a once proud republic.

The Detroit News, July 25, 2012

Part 4

Postscript

The Unpublished Column

As of this writing, the year 2020 stands to be the most consequential of the first decade of the twenty-first century, including 2001. In September of the latter year, this nation was grievously attacked by foreign terrorists. This year, we have experienced not only a global pandemic but also rioting, looting, and other violence (to be distinguished from peaceful protests) that, by contrast, has been entirely home grown.

It has been obligatory for media coverage of the protests, as well as the subsequent violence, to invoke the death of George Floyd in Minneapolis on Memorial Day. But truth be told, what happened to Mr. Floyd affords no explanation, and certainly no justification, for the mindless violence that has dishonored his memory. Indeed, as Abraham Lincoln once observed, "There is no grievance that is a fit object of redress by mob law." Of course, it would be unfair to compare any contemporary politician to Lincoln. Even at twenty-eight years of age, when he made the preceding observation, Lincoln was as close as this nation has come to producing a political prodigy, someone the likes of whom we have not seen since. Nevertheless, it is disheartening that so many contemporary politicians have misplaced their voices in the face of recent examples of mob law.

It has been equally obligatory, but wholly predictable, for media coverage to frame Mr. Floyd's death in racial terms despite any evidence that the police officers involved were motivated by racial animus. Such evidence subsequently may be revealed, but its absence did not prevent the media's rush to judgment in that regard, apparently finding sufficient evidence in the fact that Mr. Floyd was black and the four police officers were not. However, what happened to

Mr. Floyd would have been no less inexcusable, no less reprehensible, had he been white and the police officers black.

If the political left is to be criticized for its cowardice in the face of recent urban violence and lawlessness, the political right is to be criticized for its reflexive defense of law enforcement. To say that the majority of police officers in this country are dedicated public servants is both true and quite irrelevant. To a civilian, all police officers look alike: they wear the same uniform and badge, carry the same weapon, and wield the same awesome authority. There is no efficacious means by which a civilian, when going about his or her daily life, may distinguish a good, decent police officer from one who is unworthy to wear the uniform.

But it may be supposed that police officers themselves do know of the bad actors among them. If this supposition be accurate, then decent police officers have a paramount self-interest in purging from among their ranks those who bring upon law enforcement not only disrepute but also the suspicions of civilians who may, as an act of self-preservation, avoid contact with all those who wear the uniform. After all, no civilian ever should die at the hands of those who are sworn to serve and protect them, not when the civilian is unarmed, is not resisting arrest, and is confronted in broad daylight about an alleged offense that is both minor and nonviolent.

In July of 2015, former Maryland governor and then Democratic presidential candidate Martin O'Malley felt compelled to apologize for having uttered the seemingly innocuous statement that "Black lives matter, white lives matter, all lives matter." One may be forgiven for having thought that those who aspired to lead our nation could sink no lower. In fact, O'Malley's capitulation was but a precursor of—indeed it emboldened—the politics of social justice and victimhood that now has sprung into full view.

Yet our nation, though far from perfect, remains the most commendable in all the world.

Sir Francis Bacon concluded his 1626 novel *The New Atlantis* by observing that "the rest was not perfected." The same may be said of this column.

About the Author

Frederick Headen was born in, and has been a lifelong resident of, Michigan. He received his bachelor's degree in political philosophy from James Madison College at Michigan State University, a master's degree in labor and industrial relations, also from Michigan State University, and a law degree from the Thomas M. Cooley Law School.

He worked for sixteen years at a private sector think tank and has held various positions during a twenty-five-year career in Michigan state government including senior legal counsel to former governor Rick Snyder and legal advisor to four consecutive Michigan state treasurers.

He resides in Haslett, Michigan, with his wife, Susan, and their cat, Stanley McFadden.

Printed in the USA
CPSIA information can be obtained
at www.ICGtesting.com
LVHW091710031023
759776LV00001B/238